Travels in India

AWAIS HUSSAIN

v. 1.1.0
published 18-06-2018

cover design by
Shivani Paresh Parasnis

"You can't cross the sea merely by standing and staring at the water."

—Rabindranath Tagore

Contents

Introduction	1
My Fellowship Application	5
India Reflection Part I	11
My First Experience With Vipassana	31
At the Wagha Border	41
Spirituality for Sceptics	53
10 Lessons I learned While Travelling	65
The Cost of Rules	81
My Big Uncle	91
Sheikh Saab	95
India Reflection Part II	109
Back In London	133

Travels in India

INTRODUCTION

It was the winter of 2014. I was busy working on my senior thesis and putting the pieces in place for *Unspoken*, a long form spoken word project I worked on with a phenomenal team of spoken word poets. Other Harvard students were working hard too—recruiting, accepting jobs at Goldman Sachs or Google. They were on the cusp of thinking about adult concepts like salaries and rent payments, and preparing for the next stages of their lives.

Few of their choices appealed to me. I had seen enough from older students to know that working for two years at Morgan Stanley was a great way to crush one's spirit, and even at big tech companies (save for the brilliant few) most people felt like they were doing smart-code-monkey grunt work on some small feature, rather than preparing themselves, emotionally or philosophically, for meaningful impact in the world.

I also felt that the Harvard bubble had very thick walls, and the last thing I wanted to do was to place myself in another environment (tech, finance, consulting, grad school) where I would be surrounded by exactly the same kinds of people. Not to say that there is anything wrong with the people I met at Harvard—in fact, most of them were inspirationally brilliant, caring and courageous—but I felt I had spent far too much time reading books and theorising. At Harvard I was in a safe environment where all the essential struggles of life were taken care of. It didn't feel like the real world.

I had in me the recurring nightmarish vision of evolving into a 35 year-old in a board room who had had exactly the same trajectory and life experience as everyone else in that room—and thereby propagating the same ideological flaws which have led to products like IoT toothbrushes, $4000 toasters, and Collateralised Debt Obligations. I worried that increasing my expenses too quickly after college would tie me down to a lifestyle and mindset that I would never be able to escape. I worried that if I continued down the same path, I would be unable to understand the struggles ordinary people faced, and I would turn into a narrowly-focused specialist whose major contribution to the world would be along some tiny intersection of technologically unambitious solutions to first world problems.

That was not an outcome I wanted.

At Harvard we often spoke about making the world a better place. The ethical drive to do good felt like it was directly at odds with many of the career options I was being offered, which promised that I could trade time and knowledge for money and status, but little else. In my senior year I barely engaged in any post-college career activity because so much of it seemed uninteresting.

I felt a responsibility, as a result of the opportunities I had been given, to contribute what I could to the world, and I couldn't see how to do that if I went from one comfort zone to another. If I accepted the invitation to remain in "elite" society, I worried that I might develop a worldview which was blind to the majority of the "world" it was purporting to serve. I suppose also, given the climate within Harvard, I took it as a given that in later life I would be given power if I ever asked for it, and therefore it was important for me to establish inside myself, a strong and diverse belief system, rather than one which was cloistered and safe. The final contributing factor was that I was yearning for something different. I had spent four years at Harvard debating and living in a world of difficult, abstract ideas—I yearned for something more concrete.

I can write now with a context that I didn't have when graduating college. Since then I have been able to visit India and Pakistan, and get a broader sense of the world as it exists beyond Western developed countries. I have learned about the rich, extensive cultural history of India, where Diwali was being celebrated long before the West came out of darkness. I learned about the myths of the Ramayana and the Mahabharata, and the spiritual guidance contained within the Bhagavad Gita. I have also, and this was never my intention at the outset, been able to appreciate a little more the journey that my family has had to take for me to get to where I am. My parents spent their childhoods in rural Pakistani villages, I spent mine in an English speaking country where I had access to an education, and a chance to excel academically. Hopefully my children will have access to even more.

Having seen just how big and expansive "the world" actually is, I am also much less ambitious now, and less inclined to believe that "changing the world" is a worthwhile goal at all.

Three years after graduating, I now finally understand myself to be a domino in a chain rather than a freestanding monolith.

I am pleased to have been able to encounter so many of the things I set out to. I have seen the banks of the Ganges and rowed a boat across that sacred river before sunrise. I have met genuine Sadhus and have crossed paths with more false Godmen than I would care for in one lifetime, let alone a re-incarnated one. I have sat at the border between Pakistan and India and pondered firsthand what it meant for two countries to be born from a religious divide. I have come to understand the mythologies of several disparate countries, and seen the unbroken line which connects a modern-day culture to its origin story.

Going to India was, in hindsight, much less difficult than returning to London. The big challenge I faced upon return was how to reconcile the lessons I had learned in India with a Western culture that had none of the same traditions, rituals, or common myths that I had experienced abroad. I wondered whether such a reconciliation was even possible. Trying to shift an entire culture feels like tying a rope to a mountain and pulling. The harder I pull the closer we get, but I am the one moving.

This book is a collection of the writings I produced while travelling. Reading it back, much of the writing feels disjointed and inadequate in comparison to what I actually experienced, but it is a start, and I am overwhelmingly pleased that this book exists. I am sure I have already forgotten more than I have been able to write down, but, like any good meditator knows, it is ok to let thoughts and ideas flow by and evaporate, because the best ones will always find their way back.

I hope you enjoy reading.

MY FELLOWSHIP APPLICATION

My travels would not have been possible without a generous fellowship from Harvard—one of several on offer for graduating seniors. My application essay for the Benjamin Trustman Fellowship, which I gratefully won is printed below in full. Reading back over it now, I can't help but feel a sense of naivety coursing through it—it feels lofty in a way that is primed for collapse.

I. MULTITUDES

Western philosophy begins in the singular. Unity. The "rational individual" as Aristotle proclaimed millennia ago. The singular, Cartesian 'I', upon which all else is built. Christianity takes a trinity and makes it One.

Indian tradition begins in multitudes; with the idea that God and man are not singularities, but diversities. God cannot be singularly represented and so must have thousands of avatars. People of all religions have lived in India intertwined for centuries —hundreds of colors, rituals, and traditions glaze the streets.

My own life has felt similarly multitudinal. I am studying physics and philosophy, but I am also a spoken word poet and visual artist. You will find me reading from Ezra Pound just as frequently as from Descartes, Rousseau, or Rembrandt. For my piece in the Harvard Student Art Show I carved a sculpture out of cardboard, and called it 'Poverty' to communicate that beauty is accessible with even the cheapest materials. When I led graphic design for a Harvard UC presidential campaign last year, I learned about how the precision of philosophical thought is transferable to visual media. I have come to believe that these are all just different languages for expressing the same thing: physics uses math; philosophy and poetry use words; art uses images. My experience as a joint physics consultant and set designer on a Harvard theater production has prompted me to create my own cocktail this semester – a spoken-word-poetry inspired theater performance. In America, I have felt, the response to being stretched in many directions is to "pull yourself together". If you are a magpie like me, the temptation of shiny opportunities all around can be overwhelming. In India, the response is different: "let go". Unlike many places in the world, India is able to embrace, cherish and indeed worship multitudes – to tame them into an elegant whole.

II. STILLNESS

The streets of Mumbai are noisy. A continuous, cacophonous

orchestra of car horns, cow grunts, pitter-pattering feet; the color-scapes of Mumbai are rich, the rickshaws are loud, and the people are many. My introduction to Harvard, similarly, felt like standing in the noise of a waterfall—and I, unknowing, took to pruning its edges with a hedge trimmer.

That is to say, I have long sought the correct tools with which to trim multitudes into a single stream. In the beginning, I thought the key was efficiency; if I could just get a few more hours each day I might be able to keep all my interests going. I tried the *Uberman* sleep schedule (sleep 20 mins every 4 hours, sleeping only 2 hours a day), and resorted to meticulously tracking where I spent every minute of my time. In my sophomore year, despite having never taken a computer science course, I taught myself to program so that I could write an iPhone application to make the time tracking process easier and more efficient. Although the experience showed me how technology can make life easier, I also learned that efficiency was not the solution. When efficiency becomes an end rather than a means, it leaves one feeling mechanical. Efficiency alone is a poor motivator; there must be something more.

The Sadhus (`renouncers`) of Mumbai have a different solution to the noise. They have evolved to use a different set of tools. They retreat to their Ashrams and practice meditation for up to 16 hours a day. They subsist on basic diets, and find pleasure in the simplest of observations. A Sadhu has no need for possessions, or efficiency, for he believes these to be only impermanent illusions (`maya`). It is the soul that is permanent and that must be worked on, meditated upon, and disciplined.

I am slowly learning that there are many ways for diverse interests to cohabit together. I tried to eek more and more out of myself, and out of my time. In India, the Sadhu's prefer not to add but to strip away. They take an uncontrollable multitude and remove all but the essential, to reveal that there is infinite, eye-opening richness to be found in the little that is left. In my poetry I can make marbles into planets, and sequester world-bending storms into teacups. The Sadhus do this not just in their poetry, but also in core of their existence.

At Varanasi, one of India's oldest and holiest cities, the Ganges is so wide it dips over the horizon. And yet, despite this huge volume of water, it seems never to crash. It is always still. The Indian tradition understands that chainsaws and hedge trimmers do not tame water quite like soft rowing boats and supplications.

III. YOGA

"Yoga", is normally translated as "discipline", but this is a disservice. I much prefer Mahatma Gandhi's explanation: Yoga means *skill in work*. He does not specify a type of work because he is referring to all work: every action, all of life. He is teaching us that life itself is an art form, and that it cannot be learned in theory, it must be practiced daily. Yoga must be experienced with the full self—the body and the mind, all of the time.

In order to ground my trip, I would like to begin at the ISJS (International School of Jain Studies) in New Delhi to learn and practice the ascetic traditions of Jainism, a 3,000 year-old faith that emphasizes non-violence and non-possession. Next, I will participate in a Jagriti Yatra; a 3-week long, 12-stop train journey that spans the width of breadth of India. We will be accompanied by Indian students and mentors, and this is how I plan to expose myself fully to the immense diversity India has to offer. I am certain that on this journey I will be artistically inspired by the rich, multitudinous colors of India, and that I will produce bold artistic content. Next, I will travel up to Igatpuri in Maharashtra to the origins of Vipassna yogic practice, where I will spend at least month in a meditative Ashram. This is precisely the kind of stillness I have been searching for. By this stage, I hope to be grounded enough on Indian soil to converse more informally with the locals and seek out my own Guru for the remaining 9 months.

In my editorial column for The Harvard Crimson this semester, I wrote an article called *Safety Nets* where I argued that the average college student is much too risk-averse. At a point in his (or her) life, when he should be challenging himself and bungee jumping head-first into the unknown, he is too content with well-trodden paths and promises of security. When I return, I hope to do so with a set of experiences that are completely different from those around me. Instead of generic tech internships, first-world problems, and resume-lines, I will come back with an arsenal of personal, human, visceral stories. This is the how I hope to bring art and philosophy to the world of science and technology. I see the decision to go to India as a significant risk, and this fellowship will, I hope, serve as a welcome safety net to catch me when I leap.

INDIA REFLECTION PART I

It is the first time I am crossing the bridge at Lakshman Jhula. The bridge is at most 3 feet wide, a hundred metres long, and it is one of the ricketiest I have seen. It hangs from thin metal wires attached to the two pillars at each end. It looks stable enough, but sways gently in the wind. The bridge hangs above crystal clear blue Ganges—we are still in the mountains, where the water flows fast and is not yet dirty. On this bridge walk people of all costumes, wearing blue, green, orange, purple—this is India. But the three foot wide bridge does not carry only people; there are also cows, and the noisy beeps of scooters. A family of monkeys have made a home in the thin metal wires, and will climb all over—occasionally jumping down onto the walkway, occasionally grabbing on to loose hanging camera straps or baring their teeth at peanut-munching-tourists.

**

When I first arrived, India looked a mess. I noticed that

everything which was not ceaselessly cleaned would soon be covered in a thick layer of dust. There was rubbish on the streets, and this was true even in more well developed areas. The roads, to Western eyes, looked absolutely chaotic. If not for the potholes and bumpy road surfaces, then for the sounds: humming, purring, honking and grunting; and thirdly for all the motorcycles, bikes, cars and rickshaws zigzagging their way across lane markings that have long since faded. I also felt a sense of physicality—people generally queue up politely to pass through the security gates at train stations, but there were many times when I had to forcefully push myself through a crowd to buy a ticket, or forcibly eject myself from a train to avoid missing my stop. In India there are many, many people and there is not so much personal space.

But a friend reminded me that just because something looks to the untrained eye as though it doesn't have rules, does not mean that there are no rules. There is a chance that the rules exist, but that they work in ways that are incomprehensible to the naive newcomer. Understanding is not just given out, it needs to be earned. For example, the traffic rules in Delhi, once learned, are quite simple: drive mostly on the left, overtake on the right. Sound your horn whenever you are behind someone and intend to overtake them. If you are in the right lane and speeding past someone in the left, sound your horn to let them know you are there, traffic lights only offer suggestions, not commands. These rules create a very different set of road conditions than in the West. There is no rule, for instance, to stay in one lane, or to 'get in lane' early before turning, or to signal that you will be turning soon. But so long as the rules are understood by the relevant parties, things work; and in India, somehow it works.

**

I go for a late night walk in Delhi, where late night is about 11 p.m. Most of the people in this area are preparing to sleep, but this means that a whole different class of resident is waking up—the dogs. There are stray dogs all over the city and all over many parts of India. At night they gather, alert and casting powerful silhouettes in the dim light, because they know that food is coming up from the underbelly of Delhi city life. It is normal here for people to take their rubbish bags at the end of the day to pre-allocated street-side piles throughout the city. It turns out I have stumbled across one such ritual. A truck pulls up, and out of the back men start dumping bags of rubbish onto the pile as the dogs gather at their nightly watering hole to feast.

**

India is also tremendously colourful. I love the fact that in the clothing, wall decorations and buildings there is an enormous amount of colour. The colours reflect in part the massive diversity of India—it is a country raised on a completely different mythology than those in the West, and mythologies are important. India, the birthplace of both Bhuddism and Jainsim, is the root of Hinduism and has a long history of Islamic influence. India has long been a melting pot for world faiths. While cities in the West can sometimes feel grey, or uppity, or as though they are beyond expressions of youthful exuberance—cities in India most certainly do not.

I often had the feeling in India that I was going back in time. I would often find myself thinking that Victorian England, or early America, might not have felt fundamentally different from 21st century India. For example, in Delhi, the vast majority of the people I saw walking on the streets were men, and especially young to middle-aged men. There are women out and about, but the percentages are heavily skewed, perhaps 80:20 or 90-10 in some cases. It was a rather strange feeling and made me appreciate a little more viscerally the progress that has been made in the West. Ideas that are repulsive to us now (viewing women as property; assuming women should stay in the home), can be empathised with—or at least comprehended—more easily when the only people visible in public life are men.

As another example, much of India is not available online. Googling for restaurants and guest houses will provide some information, but most of these will be establishments that cater primarily to tourists. This means that in many places the only reliable way to get the best prices, and find the best food, is to talk to people face-to-face, just like in the olden days. In principle this kind of forced interaction is a blissful release from the monopolising forces of modern day technology—and it is—but it also means wild goose chases, hidden (or not so hidden) agendas, and false information. A waiter once told me that a journey of only 10-minutes walking (according to Google maps) was at least 45 minutes away! I would have been very sad that day if I had followed his advice.

**

A friend I stayed with in Mumbai has a 24/7 personal servant. This is not uncommon for people in the Indian middle-classes. We'll call his servant Chippu, and Chippu is maybe 22 years-old. Chippu cleans the house, does the laundry, cooks beautiful meals (his specialty is Chinese food), and is also a reliable morning alarm clock and nighttime warm milk distributor. Chippu will go down to the local shops anytime you need anything and will occasionally accompany us on walks through the city or afternoon coffee runs. He is on the one hand a trusted, reliable friend, and on the other is completely paid for in a way that insults Western notions of friendship.

**

The process of re-learning in India has been monumental, and especially so with simple truths I already know—for example, the statement "Vegetables grow in the ground." It's a statement that is almost too plain to warrant consideration. However, in India, carrots are sold on street carts where they sit in piles, often still tickled in dirt. In India, I am encouraged to understand at a more physical level that there is a supply chain involving a number of people, who each carry a certain leg of the responsibility for getting the carrots from the ground in which they grow, to the cart from which I buy them. I can understand that there is a farmer in a village not more than a few hours away who grows the carrots; he probably has relatives and children working in the city. Then there is a man, likely with an open topped truck (similar to the ones I see on the roads) who carries the carrots from where they are grown to where local sellers collect them. If I am being ambitious, I imagine that I might be able to keep the entire process in my mind at one time.

This stands in stark contrast to life back home in London, or in the USA, where when laying eyes upon some garden peas being sold at the supermarket, I first see the packaging, the price tag, the bar code, and then the peas. Implicitly I am being told that someone had to make the plastic wrapping, someone once decided what the barcode for this product would be and cross referenced it against every other product sold. Someone needed to print the sticker which is stuck on the plastic wrapping. And I see, in fluorescent glory, that all of these processes had to happen at huge scale. The lesson is that there were likely $100,000 machines involved at multiple stages in this process, most of which I cannot hope to understand, and so the product which reaches me feels detached from nature. I know on an intellectual level that these peas were once on a plant in the ground, but the Styrofoam and plastic container which sits in my hand does not encourage me to feel this truth at a physical, experiential level.

**

I am at a yoga class in Rishikesh. The instructor is a well-built man in his early thirties. He begins the class by making a prayer to the river Ganges, and from where he is stood at the front of the yoga classroom, "mother Ganges" is about 20 paces away, we are incredibly close. The yoga studio is small and not at all glamorous—a low ceilinged place that can accommodate only 8 tightly-packed-together students. The instructor spends almost 10 minutes in the first pose—mountain pose, or "standing up" to the casual observer. He explains how to stand, how to position the spine, how to position the lower spine, how to position the shoulder blades, how to stretch the toes properly, where to locate the bodyweight, where to focus the attention. This is probably one of the best yoga classes I have ever been to—he charges 200 rupees (about $3) for the two hour class.

**

Re-learning is also often a case of adding flesh to ideas that were once blurry. For example, the vague statement that "education is empowering" is something I have always believed, but only in a distant way, or as it applied to people who are very similar to me. I know education is empowering—it gives people jobs, and the ability to think critically, and the skills to access information, but what are the more concrete benefits? When we were in the Seema Puri slum in Delhi, listening to mothers talking about their children (we were visiting families with children who had development disorders, cerebral palsy, amputations, and the like)—they could not go beyond 'physically challenged' or 'mentally retarded' when offering diagnoses of the problems their children were facing.

In front of me was a mother who cared desperately for her child and wished more than the world for him, but she did not have the access or knowledge to effectively convey this care. She was never taught about motor neurons and synapses, and so she could not hope to understand her son's illness at the level of those things. There is something immensely valuable lost when people do not have access to the education they need to flourish.

**

Walking around Dharavi—the biggest slum in Mumbai—I noticed a few things I didn't expect. Everyone has mobile phones, mobile phones are cheap; everyone has televisions, televisions are cheap; everyone has radios, radios are cheap. No one has land, people live on top of each other and sleep in their workshops, and the roads are narrow and smelly. To a stranger's lungs, there is barely room to breathe. No one has space, space is expensive.

It is easy to assume that when people are poor they give up luxuries and entertainment for survival. But sometimes technology is so cheap that people are able to enjoy "luxuries" like music, film and television over the 3G connection on their phones, even when the more basic things like space and sanitation are missing.

**

I witnessed myself change in the four years I had been at Harvard, and I noticed that the ways in which I changed could not have been anticipated before the fact. I was changed by my environment in ways I could not control, but I was grateful for those changes.

The idea that we control our destinies is one I am losing faith in. I am a fan of the American-dream type ideal that a person can shape his or her own destiny, and that hard work is always rewarded, but I think we are told that myth much too frequently in the West. It is tough to tell a 13 year-old Indian boy in a rural village who is "destined" to become a farmer that he could be the next Mark Zuckerberg if only he worked a little bit harder.

My amended belief is that we are changed much more by our environments (and consequently less by our 'attitudes' or 'mindsets') that we would like to admit. The kind of space we are in, and the people we encounter in the space, permeates through us over time, and so I think the decision of which environment a person places himself (when there is the option) is of massive importance. This is why it means so much that I am able to travel. I'm confident that the person who emerges after all this travel will be a better version of me than the person who would have been created by some other process. The act of changing at a core, fundamental, personal level, and not just on the surface, is something that takes time and experience. The self is not a project to be tinkered on in some mental workshop; it is a synthesis of lived experiences.

**

A cow's tail is somehow both liquid and leathery. Seeming both able to flow, and with the toughness of skin that has been in the sun for a lifetime. The swish of a cow's tail is an odd blend between electro-convulsive shock, fly swatting, and a graceful ballet dancer touching down.

**

In India I have also been exposed anew to concepts of scale. At times it has felt impossibly daunting; like trying to imagine how many cups of water there are in an ocean, or how many shovelfuls of rock it would take to make a mountain. In philosophy, this quality is called the "sublime"—the sight in nature that induces both awe and fear in the viewer. India has a population of 1.2 billion people. That's four Americas or one seventh of the world, and the number is far from abstract; it is lived out in the experiences of everyday life. For one thing the huge population results in severe overemployment. When you go to a restaurant in India there are 20 waiters all ready to serve you, and serve you most generously. People on hand to not only bring the food out, but others to move the food from the big plate onto your small plate. There are auto-rickshaw drivers and security guards everywhere. Flying in India means having your bags checked by twelve different security personnel, each of whom don't get paid very much but they need jobs and get paid something, and something is better than nothing. Overpopulation makes me think very hard about the tech-elite-idea that "value creation is not a zero sum game"—that building a new product and making money does not take resources away from someone else. Their argument is more nuanced, but what it sometimes sounds like is that value can be created from nothing. I've seen in India that there are billions of people on this planet who would love to go out and create some value out of nothing but simply cannot.

The size of India also expresses itself in the university admissions process, and in particular in the IIT admissions exams. Numbers as sublime as 500,000 applications for 3,000 IIT university spaces means the pressure is immense, and young people often have to sacrifice their entire selves in order to pass these examinations. So many people I met in India appeared to have no concept of self-worth outside of these kinds of achievements, which was troubling to me. I would hate to live a life where everything I did and everything I was, could be represented by a single exam score. The competition in India felt intense, and every young Indian student who aspired to excellence needed to be constantly aware of the sheer number of competitors.

**

In Bombay the main metro trains do not have doors. This means that it is possible—with some care—to stand half a body's width outside the train, dangling from a single braced hand as the Bombay wind rushes through your hair. At rush hour, force is needed to push through the crowds to get on or off the train, and people will leap off and onto the train even as it is in motion.

**

The states of UP (Uttar Pradesh) and Bihar have a combined population of 300 million (the size of the US) on a landmass of 136,000 sq. miles (about half the size of Texas). The numbers involved in managing India are huge! It also means that the opportunities here are very different than one might find elsewhere. On the Jagriti Yatra we were told regularly that in India the "trial and scale" method doesn't work so well. Unlike in the US where the primary challenge is to achieve a product/market fit, and once that is achieved the product simply needs to be scaled out over the rest of the country and the world, in India the diversity means it is difficult to scale a product even after it has been validated in an Indian market. We spoke to many impressive companies/non-profits (SELCO and Aravind Eye Care) that had real trouble scaling their activities beyond just a few hundred thousand users.

When we met Anshu Gupta (head of the NGO *Goonj*, which provides free clothing to those in desperate need), he said something that stayed in my memory; "India doesn't need one great solution, it needs a hundred good solutions." As a consequence of its monumental size, India has space for more of everything, including winners. This is different to the US, where the end-result of competition is monopoly or oligopoly; there can only be Uber or Lyft, there cannot be both. One will eventually out-compete the other. In the US the model for scaling is to first demonstrate the need for a product or service in one small area, and once the product has been perfected amongst its early adopters, it is ready to be scaled over the whole country. In India the uniformity and basic infrastructure necessary for this kind of mass scaling does not appear to exist—you can build the perfect product for Mumbai residents, but you will need to start from scratch if you intend to move it to UP or Bihar. In India the solutions to problems arise in much more organic ways rather than from a central intelligence; local knowledge is tremendously important.

**

I am on a train in India for the second time in my life, and I strike up conversation with a middle aged woman who is travelling with her husband. She asks me where I am from, and I tell her England. She asks me what I do for a living, and I tell her I'm a student. She asks me how much money I make. I am taken aback because this, it seems, is a common second question to ask a stranger in India.

**

The brighter side of the coin, at least for me, is that India has re-inspired in me a desire towards progress. Being at Harvard gives a person a very distorted perspective on success, and all but the truly extraordinary successes seem pale; even pointless. In India the attitude is that every inching step in the right direction is exactly that; a step in the right direction. Even if the person next to you is running (or cycling, or driving) while you are walking, there is no issue—the road is wide and chaotic enough to accommodate all kinds of travellers, even cows.

The word that perhaps best captures this uniquely Indian sense of optimism is "Jugaad". On a good day Jugaad translates as "resourcefulness", or the ability to take a hand of cards which have been dealt and make the best of them. On a good day it means that situations which could have been terrible—a motorcycle malfunction in the middle of the highway en-route to an important meeting—can be rescued with duct tape around the leaky pipe. On a bad day Jugaad translates as "shoddy quick fixes", the duct tape will come loose eventually and because the root of the problem has not been addressed it will soon show its face again with redoubled venom, the motorcycle will break down again, and again, and will only ever be fixed with duct tape because no one wants to pay for a replacement part. India, I have been told, has many examples of Jugaad in its political structures, civil services and social customs, where problems are fixed for the moment, but not fixed long-term. In many ways Jugaad represents the best and worst of the country.

On the Yatra, the microphones used by guests and group leaders were constantly in a state of crackling and squeaking, or not working at all, and this lasted throughout the 15 day journey. I think this issue would have been a fairly big deal in the US, where a certain baseline of quality is expected (if not demanded) at all times. A similar trip in the US would no doubt have had backups and workarounds, albeit at a higher cost. In India this kind of malfunctioning is almost expected. It is perfectly normal to have to deal with these 'small' problems as part of daily existence. The water delivery did not arrive, the internet is not working at a crucial moment, he is two hours late for an important meeting because of traffic.

**

Benares (now called Varanasi) as a city combines opposites elegantly. Old and new? This is cliché. Rich and poor? This is also cliché. But open and closed? Benares does it tremendously well. On the river banks, walking up and down the ghats where you can see out over the Ganges, Benares feels so incredibly open. In a country where space is always at a premium, Benares has miles of it. Under a mid-morning mist, the far bank of the Ganges feels an ocean away. But step away from the ghats and into the heart of the city to find some of the narrowest roads and marketplaces India has to offer. There are no cars or auto-rickshaws allowed here—they would never fit.

✳✳

One of the challenges I've experienced on a more personal level is striking a balance between 'collecting' and 'producing'. Going hiking through a beautiful mountain pass would be a 'collecting' experience, whereas organizing the photos and reflecting on the new ideas that arose along the walk would be a 'producing' experience. In India it feels as though there is the possibility of newness every day—there is so much diversity that with a small amount of effort it is impossible to be bored. There are spiritual sadhus to talk to, and schoolchildren with completely different worldviews than my own, there are yogis with twenty years of experience, there are NGOs working on sanitation and education and mobile banking, there are groups trying to make venture capital funding more prominent in India, and there are hundreds of books still to read. But existing like this, rushing from place to place, consuming tourist sites, foreign cultural practices, religious ceremonies, exotic foods, and new languages means there is little time left to sit down, reflect, and synthesize all this information.

A connected issue is the challenge of how to 'keep oneself accountable' once the pressure of school life, teachers, grades or managers has disappeared. I've found myself often doubting whether or not I am doing the right thing or making the right decision, or taking the right approach (or even being aware of the right factors and asking the right questions), and these doubts can swell in the absence of some external presence telling me that I am on the right track. It is possible to drown in doubt.

✯✯

At a 10-day Vipassana meditation course, the day begins at 4 a.m. and goes until 9:30 p.m, including more than 9 hours of meditation. For the duration of the course, there is no internet, no books, no writing materials, no phones, no intoxicants, no sexual activity, and—what is maybe most difficult—no talking to other students. 'Noble silence', according to the Code of Discipline, means complete "silence of body, speech, and mind," and any attempts to communicate with other students "whether by gestures, sign language, written notes, etc." is strictly prohibited. This means that for the duration of the 10-day course, a student exists in simulated, voluntary solitude; tremendously boring, and very uncomfortable.

✯✯

I have had friends tell me that the freedom I am experiencing while travelling is a "mouse-like" freedom. It is small, there are few constraints but also few opportunities to do anything on a large scale. I am free to choose within the space of lowly hedonistic pleasures, like what time to wake up, where to go today, and where to move to next; but these are all decisions that affect only one person. The argument is that I have been given a tremendous amount of 'freedom from…', but that I have not achieved anything close to 'freedom to…'

My own feeling is that the two kinds of freedom go hand in hand. I agree that 'freedom to…' is a much more difficult prospect and it is the kind of thing that each person can only achieve on his/her own. The freedom to do something involves concepts like courage and self-belief—it means being able to do difficult things, and also to do them in the face of strong resistance. I am living in a bubble at the moment, where none of the things I do will have significant, far-reaching consequences, but the nice thing about this playpen is that I have tremendous room to experiment.

**

Once, while wandering the streets late at night on the way home from dinner with mostly strangers in south Benares, I saw a dog fighting a cow to get his share of the nightly meal. They stared directly at each other, the tiny dog and the giant cow. The dog was tenacious, and was eventually given a seat at the table.

**

When travelling, people often speak of how much they enjoy meeting new people. It is a travel cliché in many ways. I don't think I have met all that many incredible people. I would say the percentage of incredible people I have met is about the same as it would have been if I had chosen to live in London, or New York or some other major urban area where there are many activities going on, and chances to participate in city life. However, what is different for me is that the people I have met come from many places all over the world. For one, they are less geographically centred, which can make communication difficult at times, even if the other person speaks English, it may not be the language in which they are most expressive. But, the amount of free time people have and spontaneity of action means that it is easy to 'pair up' with people and spend multiple days with them. I found that in my previous life, this was difficult because shared time felt like it was taking away from time they would have spent doing other things.

What I love most about travel is that movement has a great capacity to inspire change. In each new place the weather is different, the road layouts are different, perhaps the language is different, the modes of transportation are different and exciting; much less is assumed and it is necessary to relearn constantly. I have found that each new place I am in tends to put me in a different place intellectually also. When I was in Varanasi, I was incredibly interested in learning more about Hindu theology and understanding the Gods and their relationship to one another. When I was in Bangalore, I would have been incapable of such research and was much more interested in reading about India's economic history and initiatives for the future.

**

I see a cow taking a shit about 10 yards in front of me. Thankfully he doesn't swing his tail so much during or after the process. I think about this a lot for the next few days whenever I see a cow sloppily wagging its tail in public.

**

Sometimes I feel as though by travelling in this way I am simply prolonging adolescence, and in doing so, running away from some of the more "real" issues of life. I know there will come a time when I will need to make more difficult decisions—decisions that will have consequence. I have told myself that my travels are taking me on a journey of personal growth and character development, and I agree with that, but I sometimes wonder whether this year of travel is as helpful as I like to claim. Maybe I am self-rationalising a year-long holiday to be some kind of developmental experience when really it is simply an excuse for laziness. Who knows. When travelling in the way that I have been, with so much freedom, it feels as though there is no direct feedback; as well as no real cost to failure (except small things like cancellation fees on train tickets or the like). This can be a difficult thing to cope with and I think it is also one of the reasons travel is so 'freeing' and addictive. There were days where I wished for a more stressful environment so I would have a better gauge as to whether or not I was 'delivering the goods'. Learning to cope with this uncertainty—to be my own person and to judge myself by my own standards is something I am slowly learning.

**

I am on a farm on the outskirts of Bangalore. There is a huge, fluffy, white dog with a head as big as mine, whose tail sloshes around like a thick-coiled telephone wire. Two ladies live on the farm, as they have done for many years, mostly enjoying only each other's company and living as they do in the cocoon of nature.

There are about six of us sitting on the porch in post-sunset philosophically leaning conversation, the dogs are twisting in and out between us, and I express some of my frustration with my travels; the excess freedom and the lack of external structure.

One of the ladies responds: "A feature of being young is the feeling of restlessness," and something clicks. Suddenly I have a word to describe the feeling I'd been having incessantly but had never been able to find words for—it's a flittering uncertain feeling that waves up and down. Sometimes it feels as though the doubt is all encompassing, that I do not know what I will be doing a month from now, or a day from now, and I have no conviction that I am doing the "right thing" at any moment in time. I am indecisive even when there are no immediate decisions to be made. She assures me that the feeling will disappear eventually. Most people grow out of it.

She says something else that sticks: "You cannot sample all that the world has to offer in a lifetime." I realise this is something I already know, but I also notice that I have been living as though I didn't know this, as though I would be able to try out everything before committing to a decision.

MY FIRST EXPERIENCE WITH VIPASSANA

THE FIRST THING TO SAY is that it was deeply uncomfortable. And unsurprisingly so. The course itself consists of a rather draconian set of precepts and practices, which, were they not signed on to voluntarily, might even be considered torturous. The day begins at 4 a.m. and goes until 9:30 p.m. In between is a meditation schedule comprised of group sits (all students meditate together in the main hall), individual unsupervised meditation, question-asking opportunities, and meal breaks. Three simple vegetarian meals are provided per day, although old students are encouraged to refrain from eating after noon, and dinner for new students is usually just a piece of fruit and some tea. Each evening there is a 90-minute video lecture (taped in 1991!) given by S.N.Goenka, Vipassana's charismatic, chubby-cheeked, favourite uncle-esque teacher.

Every student, before applying to the course, is required to read and agree to the Vipassana *Code of Discipline*, a rather ominous several page contract outlining the above stipulations and adding a few more. For the duration of the 10-day course, there is no internet, no books, no writing materials, no phones, no intoxicants, no sexual activity, and—what is maybe most difficult—no talking to other students. 'Noble silence', according to the Code of Discipline, means complete "silence of body, speech, and mind" and any attempts to communicate with other students "whether by gestures, sign language, written notes, etc." is strictly prohibited. This means that for the duration of the 10-day course, a student exists in simulated, voluntary solitude; tremendously boring, and very uncomfortable.

But only uncomfortable—for me it was not unbearable, or excruciating, or "blissfully" painful, it was simply uncomfortable. And part of the learning of a program like this is to come into contact with discomfort, and in turn find ways to interact with it. For example, two of my favourite phrases from the teachings were "Let me see how long this lasts," and "This too shall pass". They make soundbites out of what it means to be calm, relaxed, level-headed, or "equanimous" as the course-teacher Goenka loves to say.

The final logistical point to mention is that Dhamma.org as an organisation is *incredibly* cool. The Vipassana courses they offer are totally free (including accommodation and food) and are offered in centres all over the world. To preserve the purity of the product, all courses are financed entirely by the donations of former students who have taken at least one 10-day course. If an organisation were trying to convince you that it had a social conscience and the best of intentions, it would be difficult to do better than Dhamma.

The most direct form of discomfort is physical. Each student is given, in his/her meditation space, a 2ft x 2ft square mat, and some cushions for support—some older students also opt for extra back support or sometimes sit in chairs. Sitting in this space, usually for hours at a time, several times a day takes its toll on the body. I found that once my willpower faded, my back was more than happy to round downwards and creak with pain, and I was in constant battle to re-straighten it. Furthermore, the mechanics of my inflexible body meant that when sitting in a 'comfortable cross legged position' my left ankle was awkwardly supinated under the weight of my right thigh, and so the outside bony part of my ankle was pressed firmly into the ground. Within 10 minutes of sitting, I usually found that my left leg, starting at the toes and working towards the hip, gradually became more and more numb.

I would, if this situation ever came up in regular life, just uncross my legs and shift to a different position, but in the depths of meditation the encouraged response to this discomfort is to observe without reacting: "Let me see how long this lasts," "This too shall pass." The underlying lesson being that even though my back and legs are in pain at the moment, at some point in the future I will stand up, shake them off, and continue on with my day, having little memory of this moment, the discomfort won't exist forever.

The physical discomfort is a playpen metaphor for many of the other pains and difficulties we might face in life: trauma, anguish, loss, grief, love, distance, uncertainty, hesitation, sadness.

But these macroscopic events, pain in the knees, numbness, do not paint the full picture. Vipassana also teaches students to become acutely aware of sensations as they appear on the body, and also to refrain from reacting to them and instead to just observe. Sitting perfectly still for long periods of time enabled me to feel all kinds of micro-sensations on the surface of my skin—the itch on my nose I am not allowed to scratch, the feeling of ants crawling up my back I am not allowed to wriggle from, the buzzing virtual mosquito on my neck I am not allowed to swat. These physical micro-sensations, much like mental thoughts and feelings, would pop up all the time screaming for attention, and when they saw they were not being attended to, would fade away.

The physical tale is one thing, but much more interesting for me was the mental aspect. In the absence of external stimulation, a student is forced to become his own entertainment—for me, this meant realising just how dull and uninteresting my own thoughts actually were.

During the first few days of sitting, eyes-closed, my thought stream was a 'business as usual' medley. I thought about the days just passed, I made to-do lists for things I'd like to do, I had pangs of creative energy, moments of quiet reflection, nostalgic reminiscence, curiosity about what friends might be up to, occasional angst, and internal laughter as funny memories were remembered. But after about 3 days of this, I found the lack of variety to be stifling. The same people would show up time and again, the same ideas would show up in different guises. The feeling of excitement about 'some idea' felt too familiar, and too close to the return to baseline that inevitably followed. Mental exercises—count slowly to 1000, visualise an icosahedron spinning, navigate along some familiar route—also proved fruitless. They were all just so phenomenally boring. If I were the curator of my own gallery, I would not pay to go and see it.

This made me realise just how much we, in modern society, rely on external entertainment, and how uncomfortable it is to be *alone with one's thoughts*. In ordinary life, I have never been unstimulated long enough to experience the intense discomfort that arises from being bored to one's core. In fact, I suspect that because entertainment is so widespread, I usually pacify myself instinctively just as the first ticklings of discomfort arrive.

One of the most interesting new experiences I encountered while meditating was the feeling that my conscious thought could be separated into different layers. I noticed, for example, that in addition to having a thought stream, I also have an emotions stream, and a physical-wellbeing stream. Although the streams are intertwined such that a scary thought might make me feel physically tense, or tiredness might make me feel emotionally cranky, quite often the streams were running in parallel, completely disconnected from one another. This observation was made possible because over the course of a 10-day meditation, it is likely that the same thought will crop up repeatedly, and that the thought will manifest in different ways each time. For example, there were multiple times during the course where I thought about my future travel to Bihar, and I was amazed at the ease with which I oscillated between outrageous enthusiasm for that plan and outright pessimism and fear that it was terrible idea. The interesting thing for me was how I felt about the idea of going to Bihar; it was completely independent from my 'thinking' stream, and closely coupled to my 'feeling' stream. In regular life, we often presume that any emotion we feel towards a particular thought or idea is based primarily on the content of that thought, but I saw this to be far from the truth. It is possible to have a thought like "Going to Bihar is a terrible idea," and for that to be a statement that is 100% about how I'm feeling (physically or emotionally) at the time. This realisation was quite a breakthrough for me, and importantly it redefined what I understand "awareness" to be by introducing several new axes to the picture.

Before going in to the course, I thought it would be a great time to reflect. I had heard before about meditation being a 'clearing of the mind' and before the course started I thought of a clear mind as being a great white drawing board, clear from the clutter of a regular workstation. So, naturally, I had prepared a hefty file of all the things I had been meaning to think about but had not quite gotten around to—graduation, thesis, projects I had worked on, relationships that needed mending. But when I sat and got down to work, I realised that all those prior plans must go out the window. In the act of meditation itself, I had almost no control over what to think about and what not think about. Thoughts would enter uninvited, and leave of their own accord. I could only sit and watch.

One of the smaller effects of Noble Silence is how it served to dehumanise others around me—to make them much more like furniture than other sentient beings. We were encouraged to avoid eye-contact, gestures, or any form of communication with the other students, and to behave as though alone on the course. When queueing for meals, there was no need to offer polite *thank yous* when someone lets you in front of them in line. There was no need to engage in small talk or to feign interest in some stranger's weekend hobby. In many ways, this was relaxing. There was also an element of joy in knowing that other people were unable to react to my behaviours too; there was no fear of judgement, no worry about inadvertently offending someone or making a social faux pas, because there could be no social repercussions.

During the course, my retreat roommate left after Day 4 and in the act of leaving opened his mouth to tell me he was going to leave. This felt sacrilegious, as though some deep bond of reciprocal trust had been broken. On the final day, when everyone is allowed to talk to one another, suddenly all these pieces of furniture are brought to life, which felt like being on a subway train and suddenly knowing the stories of all the people on board.

Talk of meditation usually leaves me very sceptical. All too often people talk about meditation with overly floral language and reference abstract, esoteric, transcendental spirits or concepts which I am easily turned off by. In fact, I would wager that it is exceptionally difficult to use words like 'meditation', 'spiritual', 'harmony', 'chakra', and 'mindfulness' without sounding pompous. The entire practice is wrapped up in an idea of self-improvement and often also arrogance. I am always tempted to rebut with the challenge—"If meditation is so beneficial then why do you need to describe its benefits in such bumbling language? Why can you not do as the scientists do and simply point to giant power generators, railroads, and flying machines?" Those with a decent bullshit reflex are understandably sceptical of false godmen and self-help tricks. In the above paragraphs, I hope I've done a good job of explaining the details of why I found the Vipassana process to be helpful.

I do, however, have some more serious qualms. Firstly, I don't fully understand the reasons for Vipassana's obsession with "that which is temporary/changing" versus that which is "eternal". So what if something is not eternal? Why can it not still have meaning and value? The enlightened person, as I understand it, has come to realise that everything is temporary, everything is changing, and therefore able to make peace with everything. For me, I don't mind if a sensation, a thought, or a feeling is impermanent or fleeting, that doesn't mean it is any less important than one that lingers longer.

The second criticism is that of inaction. It really does seem to me that Vipassana is first and foremost a philosophy of inaction. Goenka addresses this qualm in one of his lectures, where he argues that the Vipassana philosophy is not against action, but against reaction. But for me, this response is mere lip service. There is a tremendous amount of attention paid in Vipassana ono how to avoid reaction, but very little is offered in terms of how to move forward, make decisions and be proactive. This is further evidenced by the frequency with which Vipassana addresses itself to those who are *boiling over with anger* or are in great despair. I agree, for those people it helps to be more level-headed, but I do not consider myself to be one of those people. If anything, I am far too often unemotional when a situation warrants force, or else hesitant when a situation warrants action. For someone like me then, the vanilla form of Vipassana is not enough—it must be supplemented.

For me, the highest and lowest points of the experience lived right beside one another. These climactic moments came on perhaps Day 6. During a group sit, I steeled myself to sit in the slightly uncomfortable cross-legged, left-leg-numbing position for the entire 60 minutes. I had only managed 20 minutes before then. I pushed through, and by the end of that session I had immense pain running down my left leg, there was numbness all over. My legs had molted and felt as though they were set in plaster. I slowly dragged myself away from my pillow, windshield-wiped my feet, massaged my thighs, and cracked my knees out of their calcified positions, before cursing my hips for being so damn inflexible. I was enraged. This intense emotional burst lasted for about ten minutes, and then

I finally sat down in a chair outside in the sun and stayed there for almost thirty minutes. Here I realised that I was not upset because of my physical pain, I was upset because of a stew of different reasons—I didn't like being trapped in this place, I didn't like being trapped in my own head, I was bored, I was exhausted, I hadn't slept properly, I hadn't been eating enough, I wanted to go home. The realisation was that somehow all of this energy had been channeled in to a single thought: *Why is my left hip so FUCKING inflexible?* This was a moment of bliss for me—it demonstrated to me that quite often in life we can channel our emotional energies into a few small, understandable targets as proxy for the vast, complicated mess of thoughts, emotions and sensations that are actually occurring. I hope to be more mindful of this in the future.

AT THE WAGHA BORDER

It is a hot day. I've been told the Wagha border ceremony is something worth seeing, but I don't yet know about the peacock hats, the funny dances, the 6ft-tall soldiers and the fanfare. In a few weeks, I will travel from India to Pakistan on a journey that few people make. The plane I will take flies only twice a week, and even then the small aircraft is half-empty (or maybe half-full—everything is about perspectives here). This will be my first peek into a country I have not seen in 15 years.

The Wagha border sits approximately halfway between two formerly twin cities—Amritsar in India, and Lahore in Pakistan. In many ways the cities remain reflections of each other. Amritsar is home to the golden temple, the holiest site in the world for the Sikh community. The temple contains the holy book, the Sri Guru Granth Sahib, and is the site of the world's largest *langar*, a kitchen serving free food to temple goers all day. In return, Lahore is custodian to the triple-domed Badshahi masjid, both big and beautiful – the outside praying area can accommodate over 60,000 worshippers, and as a feat of

Mughal architectural beauty, the building is second only to the Taj Mahal.

In Amritsar I feasted on a breakfast *Kulcha*—a thick, fluffy disc of naan bread stuffed with *keema* (minced meat), and doused in butter. The delicacies of Amritsar are far from delicate—the *lassi* here, for example, is loaded with tablespoons of butter. The meals are designed to give a man *jaan* (an Urdu/Persian word meaning both 'life' and 'strength' though perhaps the two are interchangeable, for what is one without the other). In Lahore I got to try some of the best, and spiciest chicken biryani I have ever had—the open air 10-seater restaurant sits in the middle of Hall Road, a huge, bustling shopping district; Lahore, as an area, is Asia's largest wholesale marketplace. We are constantly asking for the water jug to be refilled.

If Amritsar is home to the warriors, then perhaps Lahore is home to the poets. My cousin tells me that it's a grave mistake to ask a Lahori man for directions, he will always guide you the wrong way, such is his pride towards the place of his birth, and corresponding disdain for those who do not share in the good fortune of being a Lahore local.

Both cities lay claim to the language, Punjabi, the language of metered rhyming poetry, Bhangra music, and still the tongue in which so much of Indo-Pakistan's sense of rhythm is expressed.

The road between Lahore and Amritsar is jarringly straight. On a map it looks as though a piece of string has been pulled tight between the two cities, suggesting that the terrain between them is uneventful—no hills to avoid, no mountains to weave around, no rivers to cross, or lakes to slalom between. It may be that there are no natural obstacles in the way, but there are certainly man-made ones—most notably the Radcliffe line, a border drawn up by the British in 1947 as a means of dividing what was not quite a single country (the British, having originally unified the diverse princely states of India a.k.a "Hindustan" for bureaucratic, managerial reasons), into two.

At the join between the two countries, two stadiums have been built, one on the Pakistani side and one on the Indian side, where I am now. What was once a thoroughfare is now a destination, a sight for spectacle. The gate in the middle of the road is a 20ft wide structure, painted in the green and saffron of India here on our side, and matched by a green and white gate on the Pakistani side.

The road and the gate which bisects it are important for me because of their symbolism. This road, once serving as the connecting artery between two twin cities, has been cut in two and remains now as a scar in prostration to the blood spilled in both countries 70 years ago. The spasms which accompanied the birth of India and Pakistan saw a death toll as high as 2 million, as almost 20 million people crossed a newly formed border into newly formed countries, dealing with the fighting, violence and heartache that came with partition.

The ceremony I have come to witness takes place every night. In harmony with the setting sun, the two nations' flags are lowered in a ritual that attracts a crowd of thousands each day. Nowadays, almost no one crosses the border because security is so tight, but I think about all these things as I'm sitting in this stadium. Shouts of *"Jai Hind!"* echoing around, the music blasting too loud to speak.

As I sit here, in an area of the stadium reserved specially for foreigners, in a seat I did not need to fight people to get to, it occurs to me that for many of the Indians here, now cheering and whooping, this is the closest they will ever get to setting foot in Pakistan. Visas don't come so easily, and few people—least of all nationals of either country—are able to make the journey from one side to the other. The entirety of what we, as viewers sat on the Indian side are allowed to know first-hand of Pakistan is visible through a 20ft square gate; a peephole into the now distant life of a former twin.

In front of me, I see a wall of people extending high into the air. There are maybe 2000 people in the stand across from me, chanting, roaring words I cannot quite make out. A sea of saffron, green and white. Flags waving. This is a sporting event, people are here with their families, they are munching on snacks, chanting loud, hiding from the sun, topping up on water and fizzy drinks.

The ceremony started when a man with a handlebar moustache, curled into glorious circles, walks out onto the road in a white suit and splays his arms out, spinning slowly like a Sufi to address the crowd. He is stood with the broad backed confidence required of a man in a circle of lions, reminding me of a circus ringleader. And then he roars.

"*Hindustan!*" He shouts from the middle of the road. Inevitably, the response comes back from the crowd: "*Zindabad!*" Having grown up in a Pakistani family, it is a refrain I have heard many times before, albeit slightly altered. But again, "*Hindustan!*" and again the response, loud and booming, "*Zindabad!*" the man in the middle is a master—he is ringleader, lion tamer, sports MC, this is a carnival, we are all roaring, he comes again, "*Hindustan! Zindabad.*" (meaning: "Long Live India!").

On the occasions in India when I revealed that I had a Pakistani ancestry, I was greeted with curiosity. People wanted to know what it was like over there. Are they as backwards as they are portrayed to be in the media? I received the same from the Pakistanis when I went there; everyone was tremendously curious about what life was like over the border. What kinds of cars do they drive? Do they also have Toyota Corollas and Hondas? My uncle in Pakistan once made a passing comment about how he knew there were no luxury cars in India—each side reading only what they can find in their own papers.

But perhaps this should not be surprising. From my seat the 20ft gate looks like a small, distant, closed window into a faraway land. I try to look over and see what I can of the other side, but it is difficult. The Indian side has filled its stadium easily, while the Pakistani side looks mostly empty, especially in the higher seats—people on the Pakistani side are still arriving. We use our cameras as binoculars and see a little into the crowds on the other side, the women there seem to be wearing hijabs; meanwhile, on our side they have pulled up a crowd of women from the audience to run in pairs towards the gate, dancing, waving Indian flags in procession.

The Indian side is blasting music, dancing, joyous while the Pakistani side feels quiet, backwards and unpatriotic. The Pakistani stadium is also built tall around the road which preceded it. At the top of their stadium hangs a giant portrait of Muhammad Ali Jinnah, the man hailed as most responsible for the formation of Pakistan, wearing his ubiquitous Karakul hat, gracefully looking down at the crowds; ironically he is the only man on that side high enough to see over the border into our side.

The tiny space between the Indian and Pakistani gates feels symbolic also. Pakistan's Independence Day is on August 14th and India's on August 15th. Two countries, born on the stroke of the midnight between those two days. They almost overlap, they come threateningly close to one another but are, as

Salman Rushdie pointed out in *Midnight's Childredn*, always separated by that infinitesimal moment—the midnight tick belonging to neither side but occupying the unbreachable space between them. Just like the territories—two large land masses joined together by the infinitesimal glue at the Wahga border.

The MC shouts again "Hindustan!" and the crowd dutifully roars "Zindabad!" I am reminded of all those times growing up when it was *"Pakistan! Zindabad."* But here I do not hear anything coming over the border wall. I find myself wondering how good the co-ordination between the two sides is. Maybe we can't hear the other side because they are shouting at exactly the same time we are and the noises cancel each other out. Two phrases, separated only by two syllables, Hindus and Pakis, both crying for the same thing.

At one point, when the music on our side lapses, I can hear a Quranic verse being recited over the loudspeakers on the Pakistani side: *"Ar-Rahman Al la mal quran. Halaqal insaan."* I recognise it as the Quranic verse of gratitude; a praise to God for all we are thankful for in this world, but strangely it is being recited by the unmistakable voice of Sheikh Al-Sudais—an Arab. Were they unable to find someone in Pakistan whose voice they could be grateful for? From here, against the backdrop of dance music and laughter, the Pakistani gratitude in Arabic seems prudish and foreign.

✹✹

People on both sides of the border have seen their share of tragedy, past and present. On the Amritsar side I went to visit the Jallianwala Bagh park, where bullet holes are still visible in the walls from many years ago when a British general decided that killing thousands of people who had no means of escape was the best way to teach colonised India a lesson.

In modern times, locals complain that kilograms of heroin are being loaded onto frisbees and thrown over the border fence by trained discus throwers; a tactic which is almost impossible to police across a border which is more than 3000km long. People tell me that villagers in Punjab in India wake up to heroin packages in their back gardens, which are then collected by those in the trade and sent on to fill the streets.

While visiting Pakistan, I was prevented from venturing out and exploring too far on my own because the spectre of danger is always around. I was actively discouraged by my family from going to the Wagha border on the Lahore side because of the still-lingering memory of the suicide bomb explosion which occurred there two years ago. During the second week of my stay in Pakistan, an explosion in Quetta in Balochistan, on the West side of Pakistan, killed more than 150 people. The numbers are mind-boggling, it would be the second biggest terrorist attack in the USA if it had occurred there, but in Pakistan it is unfortunately common enough to be mourned routinely.

**

And then, as the dance party ends and the flag waving women-turned dancers return to their seats, it occurs to me that the gate is not a peephole, or window, but a mirror. We are not really looking at the other side when we come to a place like this; we are interested in seeing our own might, our own power.

The soldiers prepare to come out, they will perform, they will be dressed in glorious uniforms, they will shoulder their guns, every marching step, stomp, about turn and roar will be greeted with raucous applause. And I am forced to remind myself through all the displays of the aggression, the cheering and fanfare that will follow in the next half hour, "That this is not for them, it is for us."

And so the soldiers begin.

**

The most basic movement is the high kick and stomp. A soldier will lean back a little, bend his standing leg just enough to get his other leg high into the air—to about the same height as his head, and then unleash that leg down like the hammer of a gun. The foot comes crashing down in a stomp. It's an affront, as if to say "Well, what are you going to do?" It is a show of aggression and a show of strength—jaan, or maybe of life. A child's tantrum mixed with a horse's kick into thin air. The soldier, in his green uniform, peacock headgear, and red trim, leaps, stomps, shimmies and stomps again, around in a circle to address the entire crowd though most of his attention is directed towards the pantomime enemy at the gate.

The first two soldiers march towards the gate, straight legged and with big, wide gestures of both arms, they look like they are barely touching the ground as they race towards the gate (this is it!), but then stop suddenly when they are maybe two feet away and start performing the ritual dance: stomp, high kick, shimmy, stomp.

Lauded with cheering and applause, the soldiers march theatrically in pairs all the way along the road, from the pit of the U-shaped stadium towards the gate. We can see from their long strides, high kicks and shouldered guns that they mean business, but each time they get too close to the gate, they stop and peacock: stomp, high kick, shimmy, stomp.

They are here, confronting the God-awful challenge of how to be aggressive without being actually violent, how to whip the crowd into a frenzy, intimidate the enemy, and show off their muscle—trash talking without the words. A soldier goes to the gate, stomps, shimmies then stomps again. Throughout all this the gate remains closed, and the symmetry of this ceremony is that we know that the exact same thing is happening on the other side—Pakistani soldiers, dressed in black rather than olive, performing the same rites and rituals.

My own ancestors in Pakistan lived in the Northern areas of Kashmir. Thankfully, they were spared from the bloodbath of partition, but have instead been concerned with that thinner liquid: water. When I visited Kashmir, I got the chance to see Mangla Dam, a water-storage, electricity-producing dam constructed in the 1960s after a water sharing treaty was struck between India and Pakistan to divide up the six rivers that flow through the Kashmir valley. As I sat in the night time air looking out over the vast body of water, it struck me that this water was in fact the amniotic fluid from which my family was born. When the water spilled, everyone knew immediately to pile into cars and trolleys and rush to higher ground—the water from the reservoir was slowly creeping upwards and submerging entire villages, leaving behind only the tallest mosque minarets peeking out like needles through cloth.

When the dam was built, and the people moved, it marked a shift from rural living to town life. In town life, the electricity turns on and off every hour, and every time the clock strikes twelve the fans either all shut off, exposing everyone to the heat, or the fans come back on, bringing respite with them. The Kashmiris here know that much of the electricity produced by the dam travels south to power office blocks and apartment complexes in Lahore and Karachi. They look out over the hills at the huge man-made reservoir which contains their former homes and farms, and reconcile this with the fact that the electricity rarely lasts more than an hour because the country as a whole doesn't produce enough.

I think also about how the rising water levels meant that people who otherwise would have stayed rooted, were forced to move, and some, like my family, took this as a prerogative to move far away in search of better. My mum wanted to be a doctor when she was young and supposedly had the mind for it, but her parents persuaded her to go to England and get married at 19. In those days, a person didn't rebel against their parents' wishes, but I think my mum was a rebel. At her own engagement ceremony she threw off her headscarf and ran out of the room because she was so upset at having to forgo a further education. After she moved to England my uncles tell me the first letter they received from her said something along the lines of "Where on Earth did you send me? I hate it here!"

My mum's father was shrewd and business minded and with his Mangla dam relocation package he purchased a plot of land in a prime location and bought a few shop fronts to start his own business. These business genes seemed to have diluted a little over the years though (maybe as the dam waters have been rising!) because although my two uncles are doing well at their respective shops (selling shoes in one, and crockery in the other) their sons have found it difficult to built at the same rate—many of my uncle's sons are still trying to save enough to move out of their fathers home. Economically, this whole area felt to be working on its own timescale—shops that had been around for fifty years seemed to remain unchanged in the last fifteen.

The heart of the dispute between Pakistan and India takes place in a region close to where my family in Pakistan lives—in what the Pakistanis refer to as 'occupied Kashmir'. Every evening while in Pakistan, the nightly news told us more about the most recent "atrocities committed by Indian forces"[sic]. Sixty people killed yesterday, thirty more the day before. Little of this coverage received international media attention, but the people living where my family lives, in a part of the world called "Azad Kashmir" (`free` Kashmir to the Pakistanis; "Pakistan Occupied Kashmir" to the Indians), could not turn their attention away from their news screens—evidence of Indian transgressions that go unreported on mainstream Indian news. This is part of the reason they left all those years ago, and I have benefitted immensely from their effort.

**

The climax of the ceremony comes when finally the closed gate—the window, the mirror—is flung open to loud roars. The barrier of all barriers has been cast open once again. The crowd is carnal at this point. Although the physical barrier has been opened, the psychological one remains, and as the ceremony continues, each soldier taking his or her turn to perform the rites and rituals; stomping, kicking, marching, roaring; I notice that the soldiers will get near to the open gate but will never dare to cross that imaginary line separating the two countries.

With the gate open we catch glimpses now of the Pakistani

soldiers properly, and they are indeed dressed in black performing the exact same dances as those on the Indian side. We catch even fewer glimpses of the Pakistani people, but they are too small from here to properly recognise—too small to really matter. The final end comes as the two countries' flags are raised and then lowered diagonally so that for one brief moment in their descent, from the correct angle, it looks as though the two flags are touching. But this is just an illusion, like the two countries touching at Wagha, or the two independence days sharing an infinitesimal midnight, the flags are still separated by the smallest but most important of gaps.

SPIRITUALITY FOR SCEPTICS

On the final day of the meditation retreat there was an opportunity to ask questions of the teacher. We gathered in the hall at the assigned time and then Mr. AMA Samy, a tall, slim, old wrinkled man took his seat at the front and waved us towards him. The question which stays in my mind was a simple one:

> "Teacher, what is betrayal and how does one cope with it?"

Grammatically, this was a question that made perfect sense to me. Coming from a physics background, it was a *format* of question I had heard many times before. "What is Boron? How does one couple it with other elements?" "What is a Boyle's law, and what does it tell us?" In physics these kinds of questions have answers that can be found by studying the relevant chapter in the right textbook.

But the betrayal question was not one that had ever come up in a physics classroom or any classroom I sat in during college—it was the kind of question more suited to a church. The answer came in a voice that blended certainty and wavering, and despite my misgivings about this kind of high-minded spirituality, sounded rather prescient: "While revenge and retribution, or malevolence and scheming might seem to be capable of rectifying a betrayal, the only long term solution to betrayal is forgiveness. Whether it happens in a month or a decade, eventually there must be an act of forgiveness."

The question itself had to be coming from somewhere. Rarely does an unbetrayed man ask so directly about betrayal. Maybe he had been betrayed by a close friend, a business partner had lured him into signing a contract and then run away with all his money. Maybe his fiancé, after they had promised the world to each other, had gone back on her promise and left him. Whatever his reason, it was clear that no one here in the meditation hall was here for nothing. A bright, blue-eyed Romanian lady with her travelling partner, and an old Japanese man who had been meditating his entire life were amongst them.

The room was multicultural, and about as demographically different as it was possible to get from the village which it borders. There were only a handful of Indians in the group, and most of those were staff. People had come from all over the world to be there.

One man, a 29-year old who had, in a past and more lucrative life, been brushing elbows with the very wealthy, used to run a company that made bespoke suits and sold them at $5,000+ apiece. He described his moment of epiphany as being as complete as it was instantaneous – on day four of a ten day Vipassana meditation course it suddenly struck him how ridiculous his life was. All of it. The people he was around, the friends he had made, the superficiality of the money and the unhappiness of those who had it. It was comical that he could make as much money as he did doing something so hollow. And so, after the retreat he went back home to Canada, packed up his bags, said goodbye to his friends and family, and has never looked back. I happened to meet him at an ashram in India but his nomadic travels have taken him to the far corners of the world. The lifestyle seems to suit him since he's stuck with it for the past two years. He tells stories of some his former clients, talking about how the only thing they ever seemed concerned about was money, and making more of it. There was nothing else that mattered. He knew all about the penthouses, the wild parties, the splashing, and the women.

A man like one of his clients, he says, can look at someone who is broken, unfortunate, homeless, and is capable of having the thought, "*Yes, I can see he is suffering, but he's not me*" and then the fatal blow, "*so why would I care?*"

Of the myriad of reasons on offer, there is one that seems common, and indeed it is also my reason to an extent. Much of the time I do not feel like James Bond, jump kicking through conveniently placed windows to escape threateningly perilous situations in the moments just before it becomes too late to escape, or effortlessly seducing the most attractive woman on screen with a flash of the eyes. Most times it is not that The World Is Not Enough, but rather that The World is too much. There are many moments when in the middle of an emotionally draining argument, or as the work to be done piles up, it is tempting to pray for a sink hole, or for white noise to appear and drown out all the chattering—and for a moment, just sit while everything else disappears. This is the allure of quiet beaches and gentle forest walks, and from a distance the act of meditation—of training oneself to be empty of all thoughts—sounds mightily attractive.

This particular meditation centre, Bodhi Zendo, sits atop a rather steep hill; so steep in fact that as I rode up it for the first and only time with my friend Raja, my bags weighed me down enough that I had to get off the motorcycle and walk the final 300m on foot. The steep hill allows the meditation centre to separate itself from the village below. On the way up we asked villagers—typically dressed in checkered shirts and long dhotis folded and doubled back up over themselves—if they knew there was a meditation centre up there in the clouds. They all knew about it but few of them seemed to have made the journey to the top of the hill themselves. From the top of the hill we could see all the way out over the plains of Tamil Nadu. We were high up in the misty part of the world. In the mornings, the fog pushed itself up between the trees and made everything that was not directly in front of us recede far into the distance.

Mistiness, as a concept, can be applied just as readily to the act of meditation itself. After the first few uncomfortable hours of settling into a sitting position and working through whatever had left itself in my mind: the journey I would take after the retreat, the people I was excited to see again, reminisces from way back (the technical term is "fantasies" and they ought not be paid much attention to), disparate thoughts separate themselves from each other and a mist begins to fill the spaces between them.

The conversations too were misty. They took place only in the periods between the silent meditation sessions. The words were airy and light as though they formed themselves in the very act of breathing out. You will hear people at meditation centres say things like "I felt that life was finally meeting me," or that "life before [meditation] was a desert," or my favourite, "I think we are in an evolutionary transition; there is a higher level for humankind to get to, it's there, but people are not able to bridge that gap yet themselves." The words came out slowly, bubbling like forms in a lava lamp. Uninterrupted by the others in the circle, people were allowed to take their time to express themselves. I entered my first one of these conversations as soon as I came into the meditation centre. In contrast to the vibrancy and chaos of India outside the gates, this circle, with people sprawled out on the pavement in the ashram courtyard, was peaceful to the point of being languid; each word given a slow, breathy gravitas.

I had been dropped off at the ashram by a man called Raja Rajon, who in contrast to the delicate souls I found at Bodhi Zendo was one of the most full-bodied people I'd met during my whole time in India. He was an Indian man, born and raised in the town of Tirupathi, famous almost exclusively for the gorgeous and intricately embellished temple at its centre. From a family of modest means, Raja lived the Indian Dream. He had two master's degrees, one in hospitality management, and another in business. Five years prior he set up his own company, making and distributing chocolates, and gradually that business expanded to multiple cities in three different states. He is now 27 years-old and finally at a point where the business is providing him with a comfortable monthly salary to live on. He's the kind of guy who likes to wear sunglasses because he thinks they make him look cool—movie star cool.

I met Raja when he was working in the kitchen at the Lazy Gecko Guesthouse where I had been staying (he also has 8 years' experience working in professional kitchens, and was here helping a friend out because their regular head chef was not around). I was curious enough to wonder what his recipes were and he was kind enough to show me that south Indian style chicken curry involves blending onions, tomatoes, and spices together with cashew nuts to give the curry its special colour and sheen.

Two years ago, Raja lost the love of his life; his high school sweetheart turned fiancé who was killed in the street by a reckless driver. When he spoke about her he told me that she had been his biggest champion; that she had always been the driving force in the partnership, encouraging him to be more than he was. It was she who had been the mastermind behind the chocolate business—he would never have started it if she hadn't encouraged him. She was his rock, and when he found out his rock had turned to dust, he did not go to a meditation retreat; he took a small bag and rode his motorcycle as far as he could into the nothingness. For four months no one, not event his mother and father, knew where he was. A solitary man roaming the Indian countryside, showing up wherever on his motorcycle, sleeping wherever he could find solid ground.

I learned about all of this while sitting on the back of his motorcycle, after he offered to drive me along the 40-minute route to the meditation centre because a taxi would be too expensive (his words not mine), and then wouldn't accept any kind of payment, insisting that he was performing the journey as a friend and not as a service. I understand that in my role as foreigner from London, I have lots of privilege and his action could be seen as hospitality with the expectation of future repayment, but I still appreciated the spirit of the gesture.

It was in this mood then that I climbed the hill and arrived at the meditation centre and found myself sitting in the strangely silent tree-lined inner courtyard with a group of mostly white foreigners pontificating softly about how much they "feel connected to the universe" and which flavour of Bhuddist teaching is the most warm and fuzzy, while struggling to refrain from hugging themselves continuously in that way that people who are "in touch with their bodies" like to do, that I couldn't help but feel a sense of hollowness—an earthenware jar still ringing after the wind has gone.

My uneasiness came first from the vagueness of the language used. The Teachings in the meditation course would use phrases like *finding your original face*, or *becoming conscious of consciousness*. The language is encyclopaedic, technical in the way that science writing is only penetrable to those already in the know. Those who have had the necessary training can understand what is meant by the equations. Or, as in philosophy where innocuous sounding words can have technical definitions, different to their usage in common parlance. "Synthetic" does not mean "artificial" but rather that the predicate is not contained in the subject. "Rational" does not mean "sensible", but has the more precise definition of a decision being made based on the relative strengths of the available reasons for acting.

After struggling with the tongue twisting "conscious of consciousness" mantra for a while, a fellow meditator explained the phrase to me as follows: In each feeling, emotion or perception exists both in the perceiver and the thing being perceived. There is *both* the annoyed husband and the nagging wife. Most of the time, we live our lives believing that the source of the annoyance is the nagging wife. Being "conscious of consciousness" simply means shifting the attention towards the annoyed husband, who by *agreeing* to be annoyed has just as much of a role to play. Much of the meditation I have done has been centred around this idea; that in the liminal space between an incoming sensation and the reaction to it, there is an opportunity to intervene. It is possible, with training, to not feel anxious even though there is cause for anxiety, to not become hysterical even though there is cause for overwhelm. But I contend that the vagueness of the language is not incidental. A phrase like *"turn your eyes inwards to self-nature, self-nature that is no nature,"* is not merely silly, or careless. *"Entering the form of no form, entering the thought of no thought"* is not trying to be expository or easy to understand.

Spiritual guidance seems to always hover at that 30,000ft level. Never daring to get specific enough to talk about mortgage rates or fiscal policy or school-to-prison-pipelines; never advising courses of action directly; having no opinion on current affairs or political matters; making no statement on historical inequities, or present day ethical dilemmas. Spiritual guidance will never tell you whether to take that new job, or how to mediate a dispute between co-workers. Spiritual guidance does not like to get its hands dirty.

Once, I was in an audience with Sri Sri Ravishankar—to his friends he is referred to with only the honorific "Guru Ji" title—who is arguably one of the most powerful men in Indian commercialised spirituality. We are told that Sri Sri has been on peacekeeping missions to Iran and has built 22 schools in Lucknow. He is also hosting a festival in Delhi which 3 million people are expected to attend (the population of Delhi is just under 10 million, for comparison). His organisation, The Art of Living, has operations in 155 countries, teaching classes like "The Happiness Program", "Art of Meditation", and the simply named "*YES! Plus*".

When he eventually arrives, it is to a boisterous applause. The audience stands and parts down the middle aisle so the man in dark sunglasses can saunter in and take his seat on the stage. Sri Sri likens the growth of his organisation since its founding in 1981 to the rapidity of the spread of the mobile phone—a worldwide phenomenon; almost overnight we went from no one having phones to everyone having one. Within his talk, Sri Sri, like a politician, seemed to have perfected the art of speaking beautifully without saying too much. When asked for his opinions on the subject of love, he entreated the questioner to look inside himself, *"for you are made of love."* When asked what the meaning of life is—a tough question by any standard—he did not shy away from it, responding poetically that *"no one will take away your vehicle and then ask you to travel,"* observing that questioning the meaning in life is one of the most powerful mechanisms a person has for moving forward in life. Poetic indeed.

In an effort to pull Sri Sri away from high-level abstract questions to something more pragmatic, I raised my hand and asked him directly what the financial model was that has allowed him to grow his company so quickly. If the membership numbers are to be believed, then Art of Living has successfully accomplished the kind of month-over-month growth that even Silicon Valley venture capital funded start-ups would be proud of. He deflected my question, just as he would later deflect the similarly pragmatic question of what his position is on gay rights in India (a topic that is more controversial in India than it is in the USA). He responded that he does not spend much time thinking about finances, that "if you do good work, the money will come."

It is a statement, that while seemingly well-meaning can also be seen as deeply offensive. There are many, many people in India who do very good work and the money does not come; previously on my trip I had met dozens of companies like that.

I contend though, that the deflection, the poetry and the vagueness of the response is not accidental but intentional. That for someone in Sri Sri Ravishankar's position to converse at the level of financial models, franchising strategies and personnel management would be unbecoming. Sri Sri must present himself as someone who is enlightened (or at least close to enlightenment) and what kind of enlightenment would it be if he still spent his time worrying about tax forms and petty financial squabbles?

The vagueness of the language serves to reinforce the notion that spirituality allows its practitioners to transcend the messiness of day-to-day life and float somewhere up on high. Sri Sri must present himself as someone who does not walk but levitates, and pragmatic language would reveal a dusty tunic in place of the pristine white gown he is wearing. His responses are not answers, but aspirations—they represent a goal state, free from concern about menial things. The vagueness is not coincidental, for what is enlightenment except an escape from the specifics of life?

**

I spent much of the last day at the Bodhi Zendo meditation center speaking to a lady by the name of Kavita. She had lived in Ashrams for much of her adult life—starting in the 70s, in the bow wave of hippie edicts of free love and world peace, and in the utopian communal living spaces that started to pop up all over the world. Kavita had a dream that one day she would be able to set up her own ashram. She described it with the bright eyes of a child as she returned to the subject numerous times over the course of the conversation. Every sentence it seemed was a potential segue into how her ashram would be able to solve whatever problem we were discussing. A place where capitalism had been overthrown, where power was distributed fairly, and women rather than men were in charge. Everyone would get along peacefully.

As she described her utopia she was brought back frequently to a period of her life in the 80s where she was most at peace with herself while living in an ashram. She seemed to have "found herself" there. It was in this period that she wrote her best poetry and started penning the 700-page book that will form the foundation of her new ashram. Her book details the way in which the current economic system continues to upset the natural human way of living. Capitalism has failed and there is a new world order that is emerging.

I do not know whether Kavita's ashram will succeed. I do not know if it will ever exist as a real thing, but there is, in the idealism and the longing, in the vagueness, in the attraction to a place like this, much that trouble me. Within this particular meditation centre I found there to be a deep aversion to the pragmatic, and a pervasive idea that problems can be solved by moving away from them rather than towards them. Kavita recognized that those years in the 80s were the best of her life but glossed past the fact that the ashram she lived in was eventually closed because of a sex scandal in which the ashram leaders were found to be exploiting their followers for sexual favours—a story that has been told countless times at many different ashrams over the years. Kavita doesn't seem to think that this kind of exploitation is always a threat unless precautions are taken to curtail excessive concentrations of power; she thinks that having women in charge will prevent similar abuses from happening in the future.

Talking to her I get the sense that she has an undying faith that things will "work themselves out." A decade ago she was gifted a plot of land in Bali by an Indonesian prince and that would have been a great opportunity to start the ashram. But at that precise moment she was unable to perform the logistical wizardry necessary to pull it off. This is not fatal, everyone goes though trials, things that don't work out, but in this case I worry that there might be an aversion to the gritty details that *logistical wizardry* involves.

What bothers me then, about the narratives surrounding meditation and spirituality, especially when they are ambitious and reaching, and say things like 'change the world' or 'may all beings be happy' is that they seem to require contradictory beliefs: a simultaneous detachment from the details of the world, coupled with a desire to be efficacious within it. The detachment is achieved by spending large amounts of time sitting still, keeping the world out, studying the self and believing that real knowledge comes primarily from introspection. We are seeking detachment from desire, from the fruits of action, but doing so risks also a kind of detachment from the realities of existence in the world. Anyone who seeks to change the world without putting in the hard, unedifying world and taking the time to understand it, is perhaps risking a painful fall flat on their "original" face.

10 LESSONS I LEARNED WHILE TRAVELLING

1. NOT EVERYTHING IS ONLINE

We have been told so often that the internet has brought about an unprecedented revolution in information access. The amount of data we are able to generate, archive and share in the internet age is exponentially larger than was possible before. This is all true. The trouble is, that the amount of information in the universe that remains outside of the fold is unfathomably larger still. Every single conversation that is had between friends that is never recorded, every aural history carried through generations, every salient piece of unappreciated analysis, every hidden pathway through town, every home remedy and local technique for housefly clearing or roadside motorcycle repair. An exponential against an infinite is sill only a scratch.

One of the joys of being in India was that I could not rely on the internet as my source of truth. If I was looking for a good restaurant in a foreign town, the Google search results would lead me inevitably to tourists traps. To find the genuinely good restaurants, I had to talk to real people in real life. If I wanted to see if a particular shop was open, going online would show me either an empty webpage or an outdated one, and I was better off making a phone call, or asking a local. If I wanted to buy a new camera lens, the internet would show me only a tiny selection of official stores and miss all of the mom-and-pop camera repair stores that existed in the city.

I suppose this point is important to me because of what Daniel Kahneman calls The Illusion of Understanding, or more specifically, the WYSIATI principle (What You See Is All There Is). The idea is that if you have a question, and there is some set of available information which plausibly, though incorrectly, answers the question, then you will accept the information and consider the question answered. At this point you no longer have a need to stay on the lookout for data that might shed more insight on your original question. I worry that since so much of our information is consumed online, we fall prey to the trap of assuming that content which is recorded online is All There Is™. In reality, the vast majority of what happens in the world on a moment to moment basis leaves no trace, and the records we take as gospel are only a small, and almost certainly biased, sliver of all the "truth" that is out there.

Additionally, I worry that in some cases, the very fact that a piece of information is online automatically makes it less valuable. A recipe on BBC good foods may taste great but the joy is diminished if everyone at your dinner party has already tried cooking it themselves. If marketing gurus on the internet argue that building an email list is the best way to reach a wide audience, then your audience will be bombarded with emails and the technique will be less effective. Companies spend billions trying to keep their trade secrets offline and my travels have encouraged me to wonder that maybe all of the most valuable information is not easily available online—that is precisely what makes it valuable.

2. SOCIAL TIES ARE IMMENSELY VALUABLE

In the West, there is a ongoing conversation happening about automation, joblessness and the devaluation of human labour. In India I witnessed an analogous phenomenon in action—the devaluation of social labour.

The best example to illustrate this is from the time I spent in Bihar. It was one of the most remote places I travelled to, requiring a journey of more than 24 hours before we finally arrived. Once the physical exhaustion wore off, the most salient thought I had was that I was now well and truly on my own. If something went badly wrong, I couldn't be airlifted out like in a Hollywood movie. No matter what, I would be at least a day's travel from the nearest British embassy or long-time friend. My British passport did not carry the same weight here that it might in Delhi or Mumbai.

It turned out that these fears were realised to some degree when the local police chief, a pot-bellied drunk in a too-tight polo T-shirt, decided that he would pick on me. When he saw me walking around the local area he threatened to throw me in a police cell for walking too close to the Nepalese border. A few hours later we heard a loud banging on our door and three police officers came in, drunk and fuming, and we had to placate them with warm tea and explanation.

I realised in that moment, that really the only way I could guarantee my physical comfort in a place like Bihar was to have friends who could vouch for me. I would need to go around and introduce myself to the local community. I had to go to the tea stall where the old men gather each evening and talk to them. One day, the group I was with in Bihar practiced a performed a short play in the middle of the town square. When we began, there was almost no one watching, but soon a few children came out of their houses and laughed their heads off as my friend Abodh enacted the character of a chirpy monkey. They appreciated our energy, and we certainly made some friends that day. This is the kind of thing that seems to keep village life ticking.

In America it sometimes feels like there is an underlying narrative that friends exist primarily in service to your own happiness. This to me is a terribly dangerous idea, though it stems from the relatively safe place that your personal happiness is important. In India, having friends in places like Bihar was such an important part of daily existence, far beyond any selfish notions of happiness I might have. We were governed to a large degree by how much the people in the local village enjoyed having us around, and so we had a certain responsibility towards them.

In London, despite the crime statistics reported in the news, I feel safe most of the time. However, in London, the job of maintaining my physical safety has been outsourced to the police and law enforcement. In the vast majority of situations, this is a great outcome, but the small downside I noticed is that this machinery lives at a much further distance than the social ties in a Bihari village do. When we began, the infrastructure of the state is pared down, your relationships with other people become much more important.

3. IN ENGLAND, PEOPLE DON'T TALK TO EACH OTHER

On any given day in India, I will be required to talk to a whole host of people: the driver of the auto-rickshaw I take in order for us to haggle on prices; the vegetable stall seller who I go to each evening to get my vegetables; the random stranger who is lost and needs directions; or the woman on the train who is curious about what I do for a living are all small examples. I found that in India, perhaps because I stood out (though I believe only slightly) as a tourist, people were much more willing to strike up a random conversation with me. In India, I found that there were many more excuses for people to talk to each other, and people were generally much more open to conversation.

London, by comparison, with its self-service checkouts, contactless payments, conductor-less trains, and general air of being too busy to stop and talk, feels much more closed off. The local vegetable salesman in India will most likely be working at his own stall, and so he will be there day after day, unlike the replaceable, faceless workers who stack shelves at my local supermarket in London.

A secondary point is that the purpose of conversation is very different in India than it is in London. In India, people talk to each other, first and foremost, in order to be entertaining. They tell jokes, and share stories, and speak without getting to the point too quickly. This explains how it is possible for the same people to gather evening after evening at the same tea stall, and talk about the same things each night without getting tired of each other. In my experience in the West, conversation exists primarily to communicate a point, and any extraneous detail is simply annoying. We have an abundance of entertainment already, through our various devices and screens, so we don't need for other people in our lives to fulfil that role too. This is why it is possible, at university to have a strong relationship with a professor even though you maybe only see them for 30 minutes a month.

4. DIGITAL NOMAD-ISM ISN'T EVERYTHING IT'S CRACKED UP TO BE

When I first set out on my travels, one of my inspirations was a man by the name of Pieter Levels, who had managed to build several successful companies over the span of a few years, all while travelling the world with less than one hundred possessions in his backpack. I thought this was incredible, not least because of the promise of freedom and adventure. I now believe that Pieter is the exception rather than the rule. He has been extraordinarily successful, and has been able to find a lifestyle that works for him, but many others have tried to trek the same path and failed.

There is a reason why the quintessential Instagram photo is the one of the laptop by the beachside. That image only holds power when it is juxtaposed against the dull grey generic design of a standard office space. On it's own, the photo only communicates the sadness of not being able to properly enjoy the beach because there is a laptop in the way. The main thing

I now notice about those photographs is that they rarely contain other people, because many digital nomads do not have a dependable group of friends. It is incredibly difficult to form lasting friendships when travelling too frequently, because statistically speaking, one of you will leave very soon.

The other problem I found with that lifestyle is that it is much more difficult to build your own skills quickly, because you are working alone, and outside the mentorship of a team. Working alone also means, usually, that you move much more slowly than a small team would, and you will struggle to do meaningful work. Many digital nomads I met were making ends meet by doing transcription work, or doing freelance SEO for foreign clients. I hope to be a little more ambitious than that.

5. BRAHMA CREATES, VISHNU MAINTAINS, SHIVA DESTROYS

When I arrived in Varanasi, I met up with a friend who was studying at the local university. We sat down, cross legged on the ground of course, for lunch and he introduced me to some of the basics of Hindu theology. The details are fascinating, not least because they present a worldview that is so different to what is commonly understood as mainstream in the West. One of my favourite quotes from the Bhagavad Gita is perhaps one of its most famous:

> "You have a right to your actions, but never to the fruits of your actions. Act for the action's sake. And do not be attached to inaction."

The philosophy runs almost directly counter to the goal-driven mindset I am familiar with in the US. Hindu theology goes back at least 5,000 years, and the key texts were written not by any single individual, but were built up from the aural traditions of the people who lived at that time.

In Hampi it is possible to walk for miles and still be within the ruins of the *Vijayanagara Empire* which saw it's peak in the 14th century. In Cambodia, the *Angkor Wat* temple complex is the most postcard-friendly, but in the local vicinity there are more than 32 km^2 of ancient buildings and temples. Walking through some of these areas, it is impossible not to be overwhelmed by the extraordinary breadth and depth of history present there.

After visiting several of these ruins, I felt like I had a renewed appreciation for the sheer size of the world. A recognition that at any given instant, there is more happening than any one of us can hope to comprehend. That there are entire civilisations of people, cultures and histories which are happening at the same time as we are, and there are multitudes more if we allow ourselves to look into the past as well. The scope of human activity is unfathomably huge. In India people are still trying to make sure everyone has clean water, while in San Francisco, people are building virtual reality environments and testing self-driving cars. A whole range of time periods are being lived simultaneously.

6. LIFE IS LIVED IN STAGES

This statement seems so obvious that it is barely worth mentioning. Yet, in all my years growing up in the UK and then living in the US, it was never something that was explicitly told to me—either in person or in books. In the US particularly, people use words like "relentless" and "persistent" to describe the route to progression in life. The "better every day" mindset that I see in so much Western self-improvement literature operates under the assumption that the journey is infinite. You can always get better and so there is no end in sight.

In Hinduism it is believed that life is lived in four stages. Each person will sequentially play the role of the student, the householder, the retiree, and the renouncer. A similar sentiment is echoed in the Buddhist meditation practices I encountered, where the idea is manifest in the principle of *Anicca* that "nothing lasts, everything is in constant state of change". In Buddhist tradition, practitioners are encouraged to deeply internalise the idea that whatever is present now will not always be present and that tomorrow will be different from today. A person cannot step in the same river twice.

I like this idea because within it is contained the notion of gratitude. If you believe your life to be lived in stages, then you should appreciate the features that are unique to your particular life stage, because they may disappear soon. You also have less reason to grow disheartened if your current life stage is not going exactly as you might have hoped, because it is just a stage, and will be over eventually.

7. ACCESS, ACCESS, ACCESS

Being at Harvard creates a illusion that everything is within easy reach. On campus, there are research labs where people are working on robotic exoskeletons, autonomous quadcopters, stem cells, and more state-of-the-art research. Every other week there is a celebrity on campus talking about a new idea, or an academic expert presenting on the cutting edge of their field. I confess, that under the burden of my own problem sets and assignments, it was difficult to fully capitalise on such an abundance of opportunity.

Being in India made me appreciate much more just how unique this level of access was, and the extent to which it is unreachable in many parts of the world. A great example is from when I was in Bihar. Zubin had gone to a lot of trouble to build a library of some of his favourite books—several Khaled Hosseini novels, "The Innovator's Dilemma", and "Systems Thinking" were all there. But the big problem with this library was that the majority of books were in English, and the majority of students in the village spoke Hindi as a second language, and broken English as a third. Even with one of the best English speakers in the group, when we tried to read a popular science book together, I found that he had slightly misunderstood some basic sentences early on which limited his understanding of the sentences that followed. If you speak a language which is not widely spoken, or does not have a long history of scholarship, then you are immediately disadvantaged as far as accessing the world's "mainstream" information goes. Language is only one such obstacle—geography, culture, family circumstances, and expectation all play a role too.

The challenge at Harvard was how to deal with abundance by prioritising and focusing on the right things. The challenge in the vast majority of the world is access. Even though the universe of accessible information is broadening every day, getting access to knowledge and resources is, for most people, immensely difficult.

8. A COUNTRY IS BEING BUILT

The median age in India is 24 years old. Said another way, if you are older than 24 years old, then you are older than 50% of the population. This simple fact alone creates the palpable feeling that in India, the future is more important than the past. There is also, visibly, a lot of work that needs to be done. 304 million people still do not have access to electricity, an even larger number are still not on the internet, and sanitation is still a big problem in rural villages. Roads between major towns still need to be constructed, bridges need to be built, and there are huge efficiency gains to be had in industries as disparate as textiles, catering, and aerospace. The fact that India is the world's 5th biggest economy despite being in a state where there is so much 'development' still to be done is a major source of optimism for many in the country.

The challenge of modernising is doubly exciting because even though the problems India faces have already been solved by other countries, often those solutions are no longer available. For example, India needs to provide electricity for everyone, without polluting the planet anywhere near as much as earlier industrialised nations have. India cannot feasibly pour concrete at the same rate that China is doing, nor can it forcibly recruit 3 million people to build a stadium in two years. Many of the challenges India faces are unique, and present opportunities to think creatively and innovate. When the online retailer Amazon first arrived in India, they performed terribly, because many Indians prefer to pay cash on delivery rather than paying for their products online. This forced Amazon to innovate and figure out a way to accommodate the unique demands of Indian society.

When I travelled with Jagriti Yatra we visited Barefoot College, where rural village women were being taught how to install and maintain solar panels. One of the the fellow yatris in my group was running a business which helped to train farmers with skills that were more applicable to the modern world. There is a huge push to try and make sure that the millions of young people in India have something to do, because there is a huge amount of work to be done.

When I returned to London, I was surprised to find that the same feeling of hope towards the future was not present. England comes across as a country that is trying to hold on to its past rather than one which is trying to build a future. In England people are worried about the breakdown of institutions (like the NHS) which have served us well for decades. In India, people are trying to build institutions that will serve their children well.

9. REPLICATION IS JUST AS GOOD AS INNOVATION

In India it is not considered a negative to copy someone's idea and replicate it in another place.

This contrasts sharply to the view in the United States, where innovation is king and there is only room in the market for 'winner-takes-all' companies. In the US, the model for a successful company (or at least a successful startup) is to first achieve product-market fit by iterating until the product is demonstrably good (think of Uber starting out in just one city), and then to scale as quickly as possible (think of Uber operating in more and more cities all over the world). The model has led the dominance of hugely successful companies like

Microsoft, Google, and Facebook. The philosophy works well in the US for two reasons: homogeneity and infrastructure.

Firstly, Uber does not need to change very much about its core business regardless of whether it operates in San Francisco, California or in Detroit, Michigan. The language in the two places is the same, and people generally have similar incentives for using Uber. In India, each state has its own local language and in many industries there is a strong preference towards locally produced goods and services. In Bangalore you will get a much cheaper taxi if you speak Kannada, and in Kerala you will escape police fines if you speak Malayalam. State governments too, will be sceptical of outsiders in an effort to preserve their local culture—the concept of homogenous, unified India was only invented very recently, after all, by the British.

The second is infrastructure. Prior to my visit to India you would have struggled to convince me that good transportation links could ever be seen as a negative. However, one of the downsides of good infrastructure provision is that it encourages winner-takes-all markets. If I am an ice-cream salesman in a difficult to reach village then I can be sure to capture most of the market in that village; no one else would be willing to trek the dirt roads each morning to get to my customers. However, if high-quality, paved roads are now laid, making it easy to travel between neighbouring villages, then suddenly it becomes possible for one ice-cream seller to visit multiple villages in one day, thereby stealing business from the local sellers. This creates a winner takes all type market, and some companies benefit massively by building on top of this existing infrastructure.

Facebook would never have been able to grow so quickly if it were also responsible for providing internet access and cell phone towers to all of its users. In India, since there is so much infrastructure still to be built, it is much more difficult for a new company to come in and suddenly start selling icecream to the entire country—that kind of expansion would take far too much work. Instead, what is common is that when an idea is found to be successful in once place, others will start to shamelessly, and successfully replicate it in others.

10. THE SOLUTION TO EVERYTHING IS NOT MORE BUREAUCRACY

In the UK we have built up such a vast infrastructure of state control, that now, the easiest way to enact change is to modify the law. When a law is enacted, the machinery for enforcing that law (through courts, police, and government bodies) is so sophisticated that no one ever doubts that the laws will be enforced.

As a consequence, many people who are motivated to contribute to their country and improve it, feel that the most effective way of doing so is by putting pressure on their local MPs and government officials. Then, when they realise how slow moving and bureaucratic government of any meaningful size is, they get disheartened and feel that they lack influence and agency over major components in their lives. Battles to change things take the form of long, drawn out appeals and legal battles between councils and local residents.

In India, laws (except the major ones), are very rarely enforced. In order to get the correct paperwork or licences, it is usually necessary to pay a bribe, and a bribe is also a great tool for getting almost anything done. For many companies, governmental bribes are treated as a cost of doing business. One of the consequences of this is that people have very little faith in government to either enact new laws, or to enforce existing ones so when they want something to be changed, they have to look outside of government, and closer to themselves, their communities and their social relationships in order to make it happen.

Another way to say this is that starting a new project in India looks mostly like doing the work. Starting a new project in London feels like first checking to see that you are not stepping on any regulatory lines. If I wanted to start a restaurant in India, the first thing I would do would be to cook a big pot of food, and then try to sell it in portions on the street. If I wanted to start a restaurant in England, the first thing I would do is get a food hygiene certificate and complain about the cost of renting space. Part of this phenomenon is the maturity of Western societies, and part of it is no doubt cultural. We should not forget that Britain's sustained success in India and much of the Empire, was built largely on its superior record-keeping ability and bureaucracy.

One of the consequences of this cultural leaning though, is the tendency to regularly delegate local, community decisions to higher up the bureaucratic chain of command. I don't enjoy living in one of the most surveilled countries in the world, and worse, in a country that is constantly complaining that the tools for surveillance are not powerful enough. The national government feels the need to tell me where I can park in my neighbourhood even when none of my neighbours take issue with my parking.

THE COST OF RULES

For want of a better word, all societies seem to express a certain level of "boxiness" which I take to mean roughly the amount of stuff that is in boxes. Packages in the post come in boxes. Tax forms are boxy. Train carriages are boxy. Cars all lined up on a motorway look mightily like a long row of boxes. Often societies like to pigeonhole people into boxes. Advertisers and electoral candidates love boxes—though they more readily use words like "customer segments" and "voting blocks"—because boxes help make sense of people. Most rooms in most houses and most buildings are boxy. All this before we have gotten to prison cells, car parks, television screens, and the New York grid system.

Of course, "boxiness" is broad but not all things are boxy. Trees are not, rocks are not, waterfalls are not, and clouds are not. Insects are usually not boxy. Human emotions can only forcibly be neatly placed into boxes (as numerous scales and metric have tried), and complex problems are usually nuanced and intricate before they go through the mill of some analytic framework. *Frameworks* by the way (just look at the words

Frame, Work) are boxy almost by tautology. Some people have box-like faces, but most don't. The containers that Chinese food comes in are boxes, but the noodles themselves are definitely not.

So when Rowan, Jan, Zoe and I decided to set out on a 100-mile walk from London to Wiltshire, we were in a sense trying to escape the box. We wouldn't have been able to articulate this at the time, but we were trying to move away from straight lines, to get off the 'straight and narrow'. We travelled for eight days, with no phones, no tents, and no money. We carried with us some small quantities of food but mostly we were relying on the goodwill of people we met along the way to ensure that nothing terrible happened. The "why did you do it?" of the trip was much more difficult to express out loud than the "why not?"

In India this kind of pilgrimage is much more common. People will walk for religious reasons—just as some people in England still do. The walk from Salisbury cathedral to Canterbury is a common pilgrim's route, that thousands of people still walk each year. In the modern day, without fancy gizmos and gadgets, we have mostly escaped the need to walk, but for much of human history walking long distances has been the most inclusive vehicle of migration. For many who lacked the wealth or technology to travel more comfortably, the slow, laborious, one-foot-in-front-of-the-other, calloused foot walk was the only way to get from here to there. On a good day we might well cover 15 miles, which is about the distance it takes to smoke two cigarettes on the motorway, or wave the stewardess down on a long-haul flight.

Our friend Zubin, who has been living in India for the past four years, formed part of the inspiration for our journey. When he told us of his 'ped yatra' (hindi, meaning "Walking Journey"), he spoke mostly in glowing terms of it being a period of great exploration and learning. The learnings for him included the one major incident when two strangers on a motorcycle approached their group and, clearly unfriendly, asked them who they were, where they were from, and why they were here. Before Zubin's response could be deemed satisfactory or not, a whole crowd of two-person motorbikes had arrived at the scene, which quickly turned from merely unfriendly into actively hostile. The crowd, some testosterone-fuelled, others fuelled by alcohol, and some just bored and drawn to commotion, got aggressive enough that a fight broke out and one of the yatris was hit with a punch. Luckily, Zubin's group was able to make it to the safety of a nearby house before things got too far out of control, and while one of the locals fought their corner outside, they waited inside until the excitement died down. So here, and pardon the pun, the situation was more like "boxing" than "boxy".

On our journey, after walking over 12 miles that day through woodlands, grasslands and royal parks, we found ourselves in front of Mr. Baljit, a plump, sweating man who told us, "You put me in a very tricky position." And we agreed, because our request was a strange one. We were asking that he allow us to sleep on the floor of his restaurant that night once all the guests had gone home, and we made this request in the middle of his evening rush when he was probably thinking about a dozen or so other issues—drinks to be served, dishes prepared, the roaring kitchen behind him. To Mr. Baljit, we must have looked like a group of stragglers. The scrunched eyebrow and beading sweat suggesting a tension between the empathy he felt or us as lost travellers who may have to sleep outside if he didn't help us, and all the other considerations that would have to be balanced before he could help.

Our ruffled fleeces and thick jackets muddied from the journey, I can imagine some of the thoughts going through his mind. Could he for instance be sure that we were who we said we were—were our costumes an elaborate ploy? If we did stay and something happened overnight, would we be held responsible if there was a fire, whether or not it was our fault? And if it was our fault, whether accidental or intentional, would his business insurance be invalidated because he had given permission to a group of strangers to stay? Would they ask for evidence of a break-in and refuse to pay once they found that there was no break-in? What if one of us needed to leave the building for some reason in the middle of the night, would he need to leave the key with us? What if he returned in the morning to find that we had disappeared with half of his stuff—would he need to have someone stay with us and supervise us all night? And finally, why was he being asked to make this decision in the first place? We live in a society where the needy are supposed to be provided for, and by going on this walk we had intentionally put ourselves in such an ill-considered position. If anything did go wrong and we ended up sleeping outside in the cold, then it would be our own fault for being so woefully underprepared. He wrestled with these considerations for a moment and asked us to take a seat in the restaurant waiting area while he came to a decision. There were lines of thought in his mind – social lines, regulatory lines, empathetic lines, and he couldn't decide whether we would fit overnight into the box carved out by them.

This was not the only example of boxiness getting in the way of individual human agency on our trip. Once, when we were hitchhiking to Mere in Wiltshire, and after waiting 20 minutes for someone to stop, a middle aged gentleman named Colin pulled up in a red Audi TT and with compassion he said "I felt sorry for you, no one on this road is going to Mere, you're going to be waiting here all night." He beckoned us to throw our backpacks in the boot and get into the car. Meanwhile an older lady we had seen hanging around giving us side-eye, pulled Colin to one side and as we were getting into his car, kindly informed him that the last time someone had picked up a group of hitchhikers, the good Samaritan had been murdered—she had read this in the newspaper. Newspapers are mightily boxy. Rather than talking to us directly and asking who we were, and what we were doing, she had already decided that we were capable of murder. We looked like scruffy hitchhikers, and this was enough to place us firmly in the 'potential murderers' box.

On another occasion we found ourselves at the top of a hill at a Royal Holloway University student accommodation area. The frost of nightfall was looming and we began to get worried that we would have nowhere to stay for the night. In principle, we shouldn't have been worried—we had found our way to the top of a hill where there were buildings, and those buildings were invariably not so full that they wouldn't have space the size of four yoga mats for us to sleep on, out of everybody's way. There were student rooms, a dining hall, a bar, a restaurant, several common rooms, and acres of space in hallways and corridors. We were not stranded out in the middle of the desert, nor in the depths of the forest or on some large open cornfield miles and miles away from human civilisation. We were only a few miles out of London looking for accommodation in an area that was specifically designed to be accommodating.

But of course, this was a very particular perspective, and reality had another way of dividing up the facts. This was student accommodation, and we did not fit into the box of student. We spoke to several people who informed us of all the rules as to why we could not stay. Students were not allowed to have guests over, ever, not even parents or family members because of the potential disturbance to other students. And when we spoke to the people at reception, any possibility of us sleeping in the common room (which is closed to students from 1 pm to 7 am, so is virtually dead, unused space overnight) was dashed. The administrators' primary responsibility is towards the students and so the prospect of letting a group of unvetted, unknown strangers onto university premises was unthinkable. Though we were somewhat disheartened, we completely understood the university position, and ended up spending that night sleeping face-down on the desks of a nearby 24-hour public library.

The key point to me in all of these scenarios is that our position was rather unique. It is not often that a university administrator, or a restaurant owner, or a man driving home on his evening commute is asked to help out a group of strangers, or to engage in something so intimate as sharing a space with them. We were very aware of our left field position and we regularly started conversations with "So this is a little strange but…" and then proceeded to describe that we had walked from London and that we had no phones and no money. It was not the case that everyone we spoke to was negative or so confused as to be offish by default; some people "got it" instantly and were so excited for us and what we were doing. One man, a 22-year old Romanian almost jumped for joy as he contemplated the prospect of doing something similar with his friends. We slept in a church after a whole community rallied around and were so excited that we had walked so far and that we had stopped at their church—it was an honour for them to host us they said. A beautiful family we met while paddling in freezing cold waters offered us a place to stay after the children heard what we were doing. They asked their parents if they could, quote, *"take them home, mummy."*

What we learned though was that the relationship between systems of acting and the response to curveballs was quite predictable. When we went to places that had a systematised structure or protocol for behaviour, they struggled to find a way to deal with us. The most obvious example was the university where no singular individual had the authority to overturn a general rule that trespassers should not be on the premises; no matter how cute or honourable we might have felt our reasons were. This was also evident at the restaurant where there was no protocol or precedent for this kind of thing. The insurance contract did not specify what would happen if a group of four endearing pilgrims from London knocked on the door asking for a place to sleep for free.

The challenge is that systems, inherently, are boxy. They clearly define what exists inside the system and what is outside. Second, they are often not fluid enough to cope with outside influences. And third, by creating structures, they take agency away from individuals within the system.

To what extent was Mr. Baljit free to make his own decision in that moment of interaction with us? The vast majority of concerns that flashed through his mind that moment—about governmental responsibility, insurance claims, and socially accepted behaviour—are based on structures that have been put in place to improve people's lives. But in this particular case, they conspired to make it very difficult for him to do what instinctively he most likely would have done in his most human capacity—offer us and our sleeping bags a floor to sleep on, provided we were awake and ready to leave long before the morning guests arrived. Maybe in return we could have helped with the washing up that evening. The consequence of all the rules and laws was that the stakes became so much higher. In order to let us stay there overnight, his assessment of us as good, well-meaning people would have to be so robust as to overcome the possibility that if we did come with any malice, then his whole life could literally go up in flames.

But it doesn't necessarily need to be this way. In India, society is organised around fewer rules. There are places to cross the road, but most times people cross wherever they like, often directly through fast moving traffic. The police cannot be relied on to settle civil disputes, and many legal precedents we take for granted in England do not have as much weight in Indian society. This means that people are required, much more, to exercise their own discernment. The relationship is analogous to that of needing to pay much more attention on the roads—in India you cannot get away with staring down into your phone, while walking through the streets, because chances are you will get hit or be in someone's way. In England it is much easier to wander aimlessly through moral traffic without paying too much attention and just following the crowds.

The point of all this is to make the following claim, that from a completely subjective, unjustified, logically un-rigorous point of view, when I made the cultural leap from India to England, I felt as though I had gone through a dehumanisation process. "Boxiness" equates to a kind of artificiality. When I came back to England I had the distinct perception that every square lorry, glass-and-steel building, clean edge, and strawberry in plastic box packaging, had been put there by someone else.

Boxiness is evidence of someone else's hand in my life. If Newton stood on the shoulders of giants to see further than others, then my view in London city is constantly being blocked by all the boxes built by giants of the past—buildings, bus stops and bottle banks. Boxiness equates to someone else having already decided the best way to do something; a bus is the best way to move around a city, and a road is the best way to move a bus around. More often than not, these decisions are beautiful; made by people much smarter, much more dedicated, and more courageous than myself. One of the unintended consequences though, of this kind of progress is that it makes me, as an individual, feel that I don't have the same kind of agency. Nature is a mystery, infinitely complex and mind-bendingly intricate, but it strikes me that now—with our huge high rises, Maglev trains, libraries of books, and tax codes—we have created something which is just as formidable, and just as mysterious.

MY BIG UNCLE

It's difficult for me to explain my uncle to you in a way you will understand. He is one of those people who has an aura about him, and the mysterious thing about an aura is that it doesn't need to be instantiated in any specific action—that's what makes it an aura. So I know, almost to the point of certainty, that my uncle is a certain way, but if you asked me to show you how I know, I'd be hard pressed to say.

In this particular case my uncle's aura is halo shaped—he is a devoutly religious man trained in the Islamic faith, and he openly displays all the hallmarks of a devoutly religious Muslim man. His dress, a pure white Salwar Kameez, seems to never get dirty and never to need cleaning—even though it looks like he wears the same one every day. The angelic white is also in his beard which sits long and firm upon his chin. When he stayed with us in England for a few weeks, we were all amazed at how he would wake up at 5 a.m. to go to the mosque for prayer before dawn every morning. He never asked for permission, or accompaniment. The night he arrived, he quickly learned where the mosque was, and the next dawn when we were jarred awake by the opening of the front door, we suspected that our 60-year old, frail, old uncle, who doesn't speak any English, had gone for his morning meeting with the Lord. Occasionally when I walked with him (usually to the mosque, usually in the daylight), I would be surprised by how frequently random strangers on the street would stop dead in their tracks—they could see the aura too—and then offer a handshake and an *Asaslaamu-alakium*. In the presence of men like this it's obvious what to do. By the end of his time in England my big uncle had recruited a crowd of 15 strong who would go to and fro to the mosque together; one of them had a car and if it was raining he would drive him, but usually my big uncle preferred to walk.

My big uncle smiles and laughs a lot. For him most things are chuckle-worthy and the combination of all these makes him feel a little like a Muslim Father Christmas. He is not the best person to talk to about politics or global affairs because those things don't much seem to be part of the world he lives in. He has some opinions, and he is not incapable of seriousness, but most things in life seem to wash over him and as they do, he laughs a little to himself and continues on with his day. I remember one time when I was tasked with making him toast for breakfast. I made a mistake and burned the toast a little too much, where by a little too much I mean that I went to the bathroom with bread under the grill and returned to find a thick layer of black on the top of the toast. I was so afraid, because at aged 12, I knew him to be a pious man and I knew pious men hate nothing more than to waste things (after all, all things are from God). So instead of throwing the bread away and starting again, I took a butter knife and started scraping away at the black section, like my mother had shown me how to when the toast was a little overdone. It must have taken a while though because my uncle saw me hard at work—the toast must have been quite badly burnt—and so he took the two burned pieces of toast and lovingly, laughingly, threw them both in the bin without needing to say a word. It is a beautiful way to forgive a child for making a mistake.

He and his wife are both old now, both old and frail. She moves slowly and talks slowly, and when she tells us that she doesn't like her ultra comfy orthopaedic slippers, and will go back to regular ones soon, we know she is trying to go back to a day when she was more; when she could exercise her power and other people might listen to her. My uncle had a stroke five years ago and has never been able to regain the weight lost in the aftermath, so now his skin hangs leathery, his eyes recede, and his great cheekbones show off what they once were. He spends most of his days sitting and staring into the middle distance, and perhaps I am projecting, but he seems content there. He loves company, but he doesn't cling to it. When I come to visit him at this house in Pakistan after many long years, he greets me with laughter. He is sitting and staring into the middle distance when I arrive, but he pulls himself up, smiles big and shakes my hand. He is happy in there I feel—had I not come he would have continued happily as he was. When he grabs my arm from time to time as we tour the house, (he can walk upstairs again now!) I get the sense he means to say "It's good to see you," rather than "please don't leave again."

They tell me that when I was less than two years-old I had memorised the 100m route from our house to his, and I would wake up in the mornings, rush over to his place, hold him by the finger and we would walk to the mosque together.

The only thing left to explain then is that room. There is a room in his new house where he lives now. The room is decorated with a mess of paper pieces taped to all four walls—scraps of coca cola bottle wrappings, sheets of coloured paper, cereal boxes and sweet wrappers cut up into shapes and patterns. The kind of thing you would tell a child is "Amazing!" when really it is a badly painted macaroni drawing of a dinosaur that looks nothing like a dinosaur. When my mum first showed me the room, whispering when we walked in without anyone else seeing, I felt some mix of amusement and warmth. It was so very endearing. I understand why the room means so much to him. He is old now, he can't move so well, doesn't have the fine motor control he once had, and doesn't have the eyesight he used to. His left eyelid sags now, lower than the right one to make him look a little like he just got out of a fight. But what is enchanting to me is to imagine him taping a shitty piece of plastic to the wall and stepping back momentarily, with a big beaming smile on his face, so proud of what he has made. He has made this room feel a little more like home with scraps of paper, and plastic cut outs. There's a Spiderman mask, and a bunch of other poster fragments from movies he likely does not know, but maybe he just likes the colours. Seeing it makes me feel so warm inside. It's hard to explain, but somewhere, this man who has given his life so smilingly to God and the service of others; who has carried his load graciously, has never had grudges or thought maliciously towards anyone, has created this small cocoon of space where he can be happy.

SHEIKH SAAB

We are walking quickly now. We have been walking quickly all day. I'm trailing towards the back of the group as Sheikh Saab is up front leading the way. He, unlike the rest of us, walks like he has been here before, to Lahore's infamous diamond market, or `Heera Mandi`. By dusk it is an ordinary marketplace at the edge of a bustling highway. Men pour out baskets of unpaired sandals, or counterfeit Calvin Klein underwear onto wooden tables, as horse-drawn rickshaws totter by. But by night it is a whole other kind of exotic—a place where the regular merchandise is mixed in with magic: newt eyes and dragon eggs. I stop walking only for a brief moment to take in what seem to be dried lizards for sale; I wonder who eats them. A dozen or so scaly carcasses lying on a banana leaf tray, sunning themselves against the bright fluorescent shop-stall lightbulb. Then I see one of the lizards wriggle, and I realise they are alive. The stall-keeper picks up a languid lizard and shows me the back of its neck, where a heavy metal weight has been inserted under the skin to keep the animal mostly immobile, and manageable. He puts the lizard back down and then flips all of them onto their stomachs like hamburgers.

Over the past two hundred years Here Mandi became Lahore's de facto red-light district—the place where a debaucherous Rudyard Kipling cut his teeth while serving as a writer for a local newspaper. This is supposedly the land of back alleys and whore houses. In a country where any sex except marital is considered criminal, this is a place where a man can easily find himself guilty by location.

We have come to Lahore not for lizards but for a different kind of merchandise. I am here with my cousins Hameed, Ibrahim, Naveed, Jahangir, and Sheikh Saab. Hameed runs a crockery store in Nangi market, in our home town of Mirpur, and Lahore is a Mecca for wholesale goods. It is possible to buy almost anything here. In our brief day in the city we found suppliers of all kinds, high-price, low-price, best-price, ornate tables, cheap plastic wall hangings, alarm clocks, and yin-yang shaped table lamps. There are marketplaces for toasters, gas stoves, children's bicycles, women's clothing and more. The city is busy and bustling with people carrying their wares all over. It is ferociously hot outside, and from the shops without air conditioning, we were offered more cans of Sprite than any belly can reasonably expect to hold without bubbling over. Hameed keeps his wad of cash and his small notebook in the chest pocket of his salwar kameez, and over the course of the day trades notes from his wad for lines in his book. By dusk he seems satisfied with his intake.

Sheikh Saab is not my cousin, but he is here with us on negotiating grounds. Hameed is only 19 years-old, he has not been on many shopping trips to Lahore on his own yet. He is being passed a torch, and Sheikh Saab is here with us to make sure Hameed doesn't get burned. At home, at the shop, he is one of the "boys" who is there to help with the day-to-day running of the shop. He helps to put all the cooking pots, stacked on top of each other like a cake, out into the street for passersby to see. He helps open the sun shades in the morning, and when it rains and the shades fill up with water, he is the one who takes the broom stick and prods the underside of the plastic to release the water without ruining the crockery. Sheikh Saab is ever present at the shop, helping with inventory requests, and moving things around that need to be moved. But I don't know who his family is, and I don't know what his social standing is. Sheikh Saab is older than the rest of us, but he doesn't strike me as a married man, or else he has a rather inconspicuous wife.

We ended up in the diamond market mostly by being swept up in Sheikh Saab's contrails. After we ate our dinner and dessert, half the group wandered off on another errand, and so the four of us who were left had a few hours to spare. We sliced our way through the city, Sheikh Saab walking so quickly that at some points that I had to run up and ask him to slow down, lest he leave the rest of us spread out like tired marathoners in his wake.

Soon, Sheikh Saab had found himself a friend, a man who in the darkness looked both squat and skinny at the same time. He wore a salwar kameez, but also had an over-jacket. His hair was short enough to reveal his entire head shape, which was round, small, and pitted; his skin was dark, his nose flat at the tip and weathered, and he had lips which sucked into themselves as though he had no teeth. His teeth, when he showed them were yellowed and beaten. But he was for the moment, as far as I could tell from Sheikh Saab's body language, a welcome stranger.

In Lahore, all men wear the same clothing. Or at least they wear the same uniform. It is as though every tailor in Pakistan learned his craft from the same teacher and so they all know how to execute the standard Pakistani man's dress—*salwar kameez*. This Adam-ic tailor long ago decided that the top half (the *kameez*) ought to be like a western shirt, with either a regular style or a banded collar. The shirt droops long down the front and back to just above the knee. The lower half (the *salwar*) is, when laid flat, a comically wide slab of fabric which is then bunched together with an elastic belt to create an ultra-baggy set of trousers. I had my measurements taken on the second day I arrived in Pakistan and chose a breathable, lightweight fabric. I returned a few days later to be issued my uniform. In Islam, for men, the chaste area is considered to be between the waist and the knee; this is the area of the body that should not be shown to anyone except to the most intimate. If there were a theory regarding clothing, it might say that the salwar kameez—with its shirt-down-to-the-knee and baggy trousers—functions as a double protection of the most chaste area of the body. The end result is a man who is completely covered—doubly over his chaste area—and yet comfortable in the heat. A similar rule applies to women's clothing, where the chaste area is from the ankle to the wrist. There are no short skirts, no halter tops, no tanned shoulders, and no bare legs visible in Lahore.

The men's clothes are all marked in the same way, with a wavy, white, frothing line dropped down from the neck to the chest, and an accompanying crescent stain around each armpit. The men sweat throughout the day and as sweat dries it leaves a ghost of white against the dark salwar kameez, the same salty residue the ocean leaves on the shoreline.

In front of me, the two of them, Sheikh Saab and the stranger, are joking with each other and patting each other's arms and shoulders endearingly. The stranger takes us all through a maze of streets, keeping pace with Sheikh Saab. Sometimes we emerge from a quiet alley into a crowd of seemingly thousands. Other times we sink away from a busy row of shops; lenghas, dresses, food stalls, cooped chickens, into a quiet side street. We walk down a sloping cobblestone road, steep with steps on each side, squeezing our way out between cars, people and rickshaws. Our guide pushes us through small gaps and between crowds of men—muttering all the time in some inaudible language to Sheikh Saab.

Eventually we get to what looks like a destination. We squeeze through an alleyway and emerge onto a quieter, darkened road lined with what look like generic terraced houses. The guide does not hesitate as he takes us to an open doorway where we climb the outside steps and soon we are inside the house. We walk single file up three flights of stairs; no different, I find, from the stairs in an old Victorian English household. They are wooden and creaking underneath the carpet and designed for family use. The walls on the side of the stairs might have had a bannister once, but not anymore.

When we arrive at the top of the stairs we are led into a room with green carpet and a large king-sized bed in the corner. We stand around in horseshoe formation, like a New York acapella group waiting for the tonal note, or an extended family on an Indian drama gathering after the daughter's infidelity is found out. The second feels more appropriate, since I am sure we are in a state of reprimand, but I cannot say for certain. If there is an energy concentrated within the horseshoe, it is in the body of the Matriarch—a plump woman who, as far as whorehouses go, feels almost too cliché to be real. There is also a second woman in the room. The horseshoe is pointed towards her; she is the focus. The matriarch takes her position between us (the men) and her (the woman in the turquoise dress). She is slender, and not unattractive; her turquoise salwar kameez matching the dupatta draped loosely around her head. She mostly keeps her eyes down, but I notice she looks around at least once to assess the situation. Our guide is here in the room with us too.

"So, who is going to do the work?" The matriarch questions out loud. I remember the language precisely—who is going to do the work—the euphemism sounding rather pathetic. And again, *"Kaam kon kaare ga?"*—which one of you is going to do the work; almost an affront to our manliness.

She points to each man in turn, starting with Jahangir, the youngest, and his face shudders as he attempts to extract himself from the situation. I read a mix of fear and surprise on his face. I don't know Jahangir's thoughts on prostitution; in fact, I don't know anything about what Pakistani men think of prostitution when they are not speaking publicly to large audiences. I don't know whether he has ever been in a situation like this before, but I can make a few assumptions. Jahangir, a teenager, slight and bearded, seems like a man who is inclined towards reverence, and seeing as he lives in Pakistan, this makes him a deeply religious person.

When we went to visit the Datta Darbar (a shrine to a great 12th century Sufi mystic and religious leader) earlier in the day, Jahangir's face was almost tearful with reverence. He told me how he could feel the power of the place just by being there, and when he bowed down in front of the shrine he could feel a blessed spirit washing through him, warming him. When

Jahangir talks about the Pakistani army he does so with the perfume of destiny. The Pakistani army couldn't possibly lose to the Indians because we have God on our side: *"My! Did you see how tall and strong the Pakistani soldiers at the Wagha border were!"*

By the time the matriarch has made her way around to me, three of the five men have already excused themselves, tails between their legs, and I do the same. But Sheikh Saab, the man who brought us here, stands tall in his purple salwar kameez and volunteers to "do the work." Our guide stays around too. The rest of us descend the stairs as quickly as we ascended them, and soon we are back out on the street, waiting.

In only a minute or so, Sheikh Saab comes down the stairs, much sooner than would seem appropriate. This time, our guide trails behind him and is pulling on Sheikh Saab's forearm and sleeve.

"You need to pay me 500 rupees!" the guide is shouting. Sheikh Saab makes no move to appease him. He shakes the disheveled man from his side and motions over to us that we should get moving, it's time to go.

But the guide is persistent. He does not leave Sheikh Saab's side. He walks with us in step, grabbing at Sheikh Saab's hand and demanding that he be compensated for leading us to the well, regardless of whether or not we drank from it.

Sheikh Saab keeps up his pace even though the guide matches it, forcefully pulling himself away each time the guide latches on to a forearm or shoulder. Sheikh Saab is big and strong while his assailant is a feeble ageing man, so he is mostly able to throw him off at each try, but his relief is only ever temporary, as the persistent guide keeps coming. The rest of us trail behind at a safe distance from which they look almost like dancers; Sheik Saab initiating the drag, and the ruffled guide pirouetting around before launching back into another sequence.

Even in the dim light of the street lamps it is clear to passersby that we are making a scene. Our march continues from the quiet streets of the brothel towards the busier market district, and our audience grows. Sheikh Saab's forehead is sweaty now, and his eyes betray that even he does not quite know how we will get out of this situation, nor does he want to be here. But still he refuses to pay, and despite the pleas and negotiations from Jahangir and Ibrahim, he also lets none of us step in to resolve the situation.

Reaching the depths of his desperation, the guide places a hand into his own pocket and pulls something out which makes Sheikh Saab step back. I recognise it immediately. It is a small blade—rectangular and once shiny—the kind that would fit into an old-style safety razor. He takes the razor blade and points it briefly at Sheikh Saab, who juts back instinctively, but then the man raises the blade to the sky before holding it gently, just above the top of his own head.

"Give me my money, or I will cut myself!" he shouts. Everyone around can hear, though no crowd gathers around us. The blade held as though the blade wielder were pulling himself up by a string attached to the crown of his skull.

"*Meh kaat dungha!*" In Urdu his voice carries no fear or weakness, only sincerity and urgency. The blade position suggesting that if he were to do it, then his body might just split perfectly in half down the middle, left side and right side, as if cleaved in two by a butcher's bandsaw.

Sheikh Saab steels himself and decides that even this is not enough to justify payment, he will not be swindled. He grabs the man by the wrist of the bladed hand and pulls it in close to his own body so the blade is pointing away from both of them. Before the guide is able to escape the grip, and before the blade can be released the stranger is standing directly in front of Sheikh Saab. He raises his blade to the top of his skull in threat once more.

Sheikh Saab pushes past him and keeps moving, the guide follows him, and we follow too at a distance.

Soon we come to the centre of a market, but when we get there, I realise we have a problem which makes the guide seem like child's play. The green uniform and black beret of a Lahori police officer emerges from the crowd, and we watch from behind a wooden shopping cart as Sheikh Saab is shoved hard in the back and then slapped over the head. "What the fuck are you doing" the police officer yells, pinning Sheikh Saab's left arm behind him so he buckles forward awkwardly. The police officer slaps him over the head a few more times for good measure. There are maybe three or four officers now, all surrounding Sheikh Saab and pushing the guide away.

Jahangir, Amjand and I try to remain inconspicuous, watching the scene unfold from twenty metres away, using a fruit stall for cover. But we are ratted out when the police officers look around and a random member of the public points directly at us and hollers to get the officer's attention. We step forward slowly. The chief police officer walks over to us as the others keep Sheikh Saab restrained. The blade is out of sight now but the guide is still whining to the police that he still hasn't received his money as they shoo him away.

By now I am genuinely concerned. If the situation before had seemed like it could be evaded, then now it seems actively worrying. I have no ambitions of seeing the inside of a Lahori police cell, and I have no desire to tell my parents and relatives back in Mirpur that we were caught walking around the red-light district. I have also spent enough time in the developing world to know that police are by default not to be trusted. There are stories of tourists in Thailand being held for ransoms of hundreds of dollars after having illegal drugs planted on them by the very same officers who are doing the arresting. In India I was ruffled by a drunken and incoherent police officer for wandering too close to the Nepalese border, even though we were hundreds of metres away. In my very first 20 minutes in Pakistan, as we were leaving the airport, my uncle's car was pulled over and he was forced to pay a bribe for having the wrong kind of screws on his license plate. My uncle carries small bills in his car specifically for this reason—to pay his inevitable policeman tax.

The police officer demands to see our *Shanakhti* cards. These are the government issued ID cards that each person is required to carry with them at all time. Jahangir and Ibrahim try to plead with the officer, using me as a bargaining piece. I am just a tourist they say, I have come all the way from England to visit Pakistan and I should leave with a good impression. I have my passport in my back pocket but I hand over my driving license, reasoning that it will be easier to replace when I get back to England.

"You know, you have been doing some sinful things" the officer reminds us as he looks through the documents we have given him, and then he places them into his top pocket. "You look like good men, what are you doing here?" We try to explain but his attention is spread thin and he doesn't appear to be listening.

The police officer says he is calling for a car to come pick us up and take us to the police station. He walks back over to Sheikh Saab, and after several minutes of same kind of negotiation Sheikh Saab is able to find a solution. Sheikh Saab discreetly pulls 1500 rupees from his pocket (triple the amount he would have had to pay the guide just half an hour before), and tries to push it into the chief officer's hands.

Suddenly the burly, threatening police officer looks like a child. In one simple act he seems to have shrunk several inches and lost his puffed-up posture. He is having money thrust into his hands but he doesn't want to do it here, not so publicly, and so he shirks away from Sheikh Saab and tries to walk away. Sheikh Saab—who is also much bigger than the police officer—grabs him by the shoulders and tries to turn him around. The officer resists and keeps walking, the four of us in tow, until we manage to find a quiet side street away from the main market where the transaction can happen. Happy with his earnings for the evening, the police officer seems suddenly less intimidating as he hands back our identification cards and tells us, "I knew you were good people all along, I could tell from his beard," pointing to Jahangir's facial hair.

**

Later that evening we met up with the rest of the group and went to a theatre show. This was something that my cousins were very excited about. They told me they made an effort to go to a show each and every time they came to visit Lahore.

We entered the venue, which I later found out was the Al-Falah theatre on Hall Road in Lahore. The seats were worn down and the theatre looked like it had been around for many decades. There were no ushers, no seat allocations, no guards to check tickets and no sitting quietly waiting for the show to start. Instead, people filled the theatre raucously, finding seats wherever they could and chatting with their friends. We arrived early enough that we got a seat near the front.

The show itself was full of good old-fashioned slapstick humour. Obvious jokes and intrinsically funny characters. The theatre was large enough that microphones would have been appropriate but there were no microphones—instead the actors projected their voices loudly for every joke. The audience heard every single word of the thick punjabi accents and my cousins were rolling around in their seats laughing for almost all of the two hour long performance. During the show, I remember thinking to myself that I suddenly understood how an event like the Rite of Spring riots could have happened. In every other theatre I have been to, there is a distance between the actors and the audience, but here it felt like the audience and the actors were almost touching.

As the show was wrapping up, it descended, to my surprise, into what can only be described as a softcore pornography show. The female actresses, who were famous enough to have their faces on billboards outside the venue, took it in turns to perform on stage, where performing meant dancing provocatively and shaking the parts of their bodies that had mostly been covered until now. It was like watching a hip-hop music video, but in person on stage. I had to remind myself that men here have a very different relationship to women than we do in the UK. Online pornography in Pakistan is banned. In a heavily masculine society, the places men go to get their releases are often secretive and dangerous. Extra-marital sex is a criminal offence in Pakistan. I wondered how much it happens and whether it is ever punished.

As we left the theatre and made our way back towards the bus station, past midnight, the day felt like it was well and truly done. My cousin took me to one side and kindly told me

"Make sure you don't mention this to my parents, they don't know that we go to these shows. In England woman walk around with their legs out, and their shoulders showing," he continued, "in Pakistan we don't have that."

There was a lot from that day we never spoke of again.

INDIA REFLECTION PART II

He introduces himself to the group with "Before, I was nothing – I knew nothing, I had nothing, I was nothing…" We'll call him Kamal, a young teenage boy turning man who I met while at Project Potential University in Bihar; he swallows the trailing message of hope "… but here I feel inspired." I think of his nothingness and contrast it to all the nothings I've known. The 'felt like nothing' of a strong but specific gaze, the 'felt like nothing' of being ignored; a boomeranged text message not coming back. When he says 'nothing', I don't sense that he means an email rejection for a job he really wanted. I think he is perceiving, more subconsciously than consciously, living for days and years, knowing deep down that he was ignored by the world and that in all likelihood the dreams and desires he had for himself and those he cares about would never materialise. And then slowly I understand the kind of gratitude and hunger he directs towards anyone or anything that promises to be 'something'.

**

I went to India with five T-shirts bought for about £3 each, and though I didn't expect these disposable necessities to last very long, I found that—tattered, colour faded, muddied, sweaty from some unremembered hike, creased permanently from being thrown into the bottom of a rucksack and never ironed, worn out from being washed too many times in a plastic bucket and dried on lines between trees, thread loose, butter chicken curry stained, soaked with the aromas of Delhi pollution, underground marketplaces, and charcoaled firewood—they did.

Not since my return has anyone in London ever commented on my clothing, or suggested I should finally throw away the old, green-blue Primark T-shirt. But in London, for whatever multitude of reasons, I just feel less comfortable wearing that T-shirt out in public. Everyone here is so well-dressed. I can't help but feel that they're looking.

When I think about what I gained most from India, it doesn't boil down to a single event or a single experience; instead it resides in the air that connects those moments. It's not about what happened in India but about what's possible in India, what's normal in India. Not about what I saw in India, but about the things that are ever present and invisible in England. The learnings from India are vague, spread out, difficult to pin down, and, like air, can become dangerous when compressed to a few bullet points or resume lines.

In India, I became an expert at mosquito hunting. My ears became sensitive enough that I could pinpoint a mosquito's exact location from just a few gentle buzzes by my neck. I could strike a mosquito down in an instant; I mastered the one handed mosquito clap for when the traditional two hander was not an option. The mosquitos here have snouts so long they can pierce through clothing, and I remember once sitting and watching a mosquito shoving his snout doggedly though every little hole in my mosquito net. Believing maybe, each time, that he had finally struck blood.

In many parts of India the signals of poverty and privilege are ever present. It is easy to walk in Delhi and find a family huddled up, a tarp tied against a railing becoming their makeshift tent; the family cow tied up outside their home on a piece of slack rope. It is impossible to walk far without seeing swathes of people—rickshaw drivers, beggars, merchants—striving to create the best possible lives for themselves. Their generational wealth accumulated over many centuries amounting to no more than a week's wages in the US. It is difficult in such a situation to not feel immensely blessed. I recognised every day the significance of what I had been given in life (an education, the ability to read English, good health and access to well-connected people), and necessity to make use of these privileges. Conversely, in London it sometimes seems that people have nothing to lose—at least nothing to lose except status—maybe that's why they take themselves so seriously.

**

I arrive in Bangalore and the heavens are open. God is sending down a rainstorm. The taxi window wipers are going at full speed and the tires are making bow waves through the water. This, I've been told, happens from time to time. The rains come and the city that was built too quickly does not have adequate drainage so the excess water gathers and sits overnight, creating flash floods and spontaneous flows. It's not a problem that's unique to Bangalore, but sitting in this rain I am reminded that less than 30 years ago, much of this land would have been green and filled with vegetation: "India's Garden" they called it. The water would have filtered its way down through the soil and on through the layers of rocks, purifying itself in the process to become groundwater. But the concrete which has built up since then is not so porous, and so the water just sits on the surface. Dirty rather than filtered clean.

**

I stayed at first in an Airbnb on the edge of town. Having visited Bangalore before, I assumed that this time I would be less phased by the chaos; that the noise might feel normal, and haggling with auto rickshaw drivers would feel less out of character. Perhaps I would feel a little more at home amongst the street dogs and animals. I was wrong. Soon after arriving, I was shown how much of Bangalore I had forgotten since my last visit. There is a road in Bangalore, called Bannerghatta road. It runs for about 4km and connects much of South Bangalore to the city centre. I could have sworn that since this was a main road (it's marked as such on Google maps), it was fully paved and well maintained with pavements on both sides, but when I got there I realised I had been fooled by the comparative modernity of the roads in Bangkok, where I had just come from. Bannerghatta, a main road, was falling away at the sides, and the road itself was just as potholed as the smaller roads nearby. At its edges the road disappeared into rubbish, dust, fruit wagons and wandering animals where the pavement should be. A sign I used to drive by everyday read "Do not urinate against this wall. Fine Rs 500".

That was not the only thing I had remembered incorrectly. In India when you use Uber to book a taxi, you have to make a phone call to the driver because otherwise he might never show up – GPS is unreliable, and besides, the driver doesn't trust it. If you speak Kannada (the local language) he'll be nicer to you; this is the unofficial local knowledge tax. I had forgotten how crumbling everything looked in India. In comparison, Bangkok felt like Europe, with malls and new buildings everywhere. Friends told me that in India there is a bureaucratic aversion to maintenance, since projects are conceived of as one time things, which require a certain amount of financing and then when they are done they are done. There is no maintenance budget.

Bangalore is a young city. That's true at the level of the city itself, which was really only formed when it adopted the "techcity" tag in the 2000s and it played to the many call-centres that served disgruntled customers in the West. Now Bangalore is the start-up hub of India, and like these young companies, much of Bangalore's crowd is young also. For many, coming to Bangalore for work or university represents leaving a family behind for the first time in their lives, which means that much of the culture of the place is still being decided. Unlike New York or London, or even Mumbai, where it is clear that there is adult supervision and old money pulling the strings, in Bangalore that same feeling doesn't exist. Here, wherever you go, at all the best events, the people are skewed towards the young side, late teens or early twenties—people who are still coming to conclusions about who they are and what they stand for. I met, for example, start up media companies that were being run to profitability by 23 year-olds, and this did not seem out of the ordinary at all. This makes Bangalore in many ways a fantastic place to be and a fantastic place to come of age. It also creates a challenge because it represents a kind of self-governance which I'm excited to see play out over time.

At the heart of youth culture here, there is a group called the Under 25 club, which organises brilliant events throughout the city on a regular basis. During my last week in the city, I went to one called Lit Fest; a weekend celebration of all things literary, including guest speakers and YouTube movie stars. Here I listened to an incredible poem by a young lady about the topic of menstruation, which in some parts of India is still considered dirty. In some places, when a woman has her first period she is put into a room by herself and taken away from society until she is deemed to be clean again. The place she bleeds from is seen as a dirty place and her bleeding is seen as something to be sequestered away. The taboo nature of the topic also means that many women, especially in rural areas, do not get access to the sanitary pads and equipment they need. These are the kinds of taboo topics that are finally being talked about in places like Bangalore.

**

Places also have hearts and souls, they do not reveal themselves so easily, they have been trodden on before they knew to hide their gems. This, I think, is the root of the problem with tourism as an industry, and more generally with the fact that few people can afford to take enough time off work to fully enjoy and appreciate a place. When I reflect on the best moments of my last year it is clear that they happened in (and I use this quote embarrassingly) a John Green kind of way "very slowly, and then all at once." I feel as though the lives we live here in England, where joy is crammed into the evenings and weekends, and personal travel holidays are once a year luxuries that need to be made the most of: we live lives which demand the all at once, without leaving room for the very slowly.

**

From Bangalore, I tried my best to travel to nearby places. I had read about Pondicherry in Yan Martel's "Life Of Pi'" but what I mostly remembered was the swimming pool—dirty water with a layer of swallowable gunk floating on the surface —that the main character 'Piscine' was named after. When I got to Pondi what I found instead was something far more beautiful. The influence of French design on this place was refreshing—the houses crisp and clean, each their own bright colour, blue, red or yellow, and all united by a white trim surrounding the doors and windows. A beachside, holiday town, where families go to eat ice cream and relax by the ocean. At dusk, the long beach promenade was filled with families— whole and buzzing in dim light, where children with ice cream watch the waves beating themselves against the rocks.

If I knew of Pondi through Life of Pi, then Auroville, from the descriptions I had heard of it, sounded like the tropical island Pi discovers when he is out on the ocean. In the novel, the narrator describes the trees on the island as being so vibrant that they make vegetation in the monsoons look a dull olive in comparison. Friends who had spent time in Auroville often described it as one of their favourite places on Earth, so I was keen to visit. In the end, Pi's island turned out to be man-eating, but, like Pi, I couldn't have known that ahead of time.

I rented a scooter and braved the 20 mile journey to Auroville. I was only there for a brief three days, but it was a very thorough introduction to what a "Utopia" looks like in practice. It is a township that was founded in the 1960s by a woman referred to honorifically as *the mother*; a place for people to live freely and peacefully in harmony with one another and with nature. At the founding ceremony in 1968, the heyday of the hippie alternative community movement, people from all over the world brought with them a jar of soil from their home countries, and poured the soil into a pile in the middle to memorialise Auroville's stated aim of helping to "realise human unity." On the motorcycle ride over, Auroville signalled itself to me with its soil—as the township approaches, the brown dirt roads leading to it start to turn a bright red. In Auroville there is no ownership of property, there is no money, labour is shared, and the community is designed to be self-sustaining and egalitarian.

At the epicentre of Auroville, on the hill from which the rest of the town seems to emanate, is the Matrimandir—a shrine built over the past 20 years which is home to perhaps the most perfect meditation room in the world. The Matrimandir is specially designed so that it channels a single beam of light from the sky, down, like a laser beam to rest on the top of the head of whoever is meditating in the middle. I never got the opportunity to take my seat there, partly because I hadn't committed to Auroville's mission, but it is where many people reportedly find their peace with the world.

For me, the entire area of Auroville was experienced as somewhat of an act of worship. I couldn't help but feel the devotion as people talk about the mother and talk about the place. One of my friends had previously spent 3 months working on a farm in Auroville, and whenever she reminisced on it, she spoke with a note of adoration about the profound effect it had on her. She described that there was something fundamental about waking up at 5 a.m. each morning to a horizon of seeds that needed to be sown, or plants to be harvested, and then seeing the same work done at the end of the day. She is also the same person who was constantly reminding me to put my phone away and get away from my computer screen.

My take away from Auroville though, was that it was a Utopia gone wrong, and a subtle rather than devastating lesson to those who think the ails of the world can be solved in simple ways. The conversations I had there were hollow—echoed somehow, as though people weren't quite telling me the truth. One woman, when I asked her to tell me a little about the place, couldn't stop telling me how wonderful it was, how beautiful she thought the world was and how intensely joyous every waking moment of her life was. I wondered if I should burst her bubble by encouraging her to be more critical or discerning, but I wasn't feeling so bold. From talking to people, it also seemed like Auroville has not been able to escape the politics and infighting of outside society. The town is organised into "units" dedicated to doing different things (with names like "Grace", "Creativity" and "Solitude")—one is exploring sustainable architecture, another focuses on growing seeds and farming practices. Nonetheless, each unit seems to be constantly complaining about resource allocation and how other units are benefitting more from the Auroville rules than they are. Even though there is no money in Auroville, many people will spend six or more months a year away from Auroville in order to earn a living.

The primary gift I received from Auroville, was that it did introduce me to one of my favourite people in India. She was a tall, thin 40-year old woman from Eritrea, who in a previous life was a high-flying lawyer in San Francisco. She had decided that there was more to life than how she had been living, and slowly started spending more and more time in places like Auroville. She told me about how life for her had been this meandering journey—she had grown up in Eritrea with her family, and moved to America at a fairly young age, and though we only spoke for an hour or so, I was taken aback by the openness with which she was willing to share the personal details of her life. We bonded over our thoughts on Islam in the modern age, and the tensions we experienced with our parents; she told me about the disputes she had had with her brother and how fixing that relationship had taken more strength than she knew she had. In a world where so many people seem hidden within their shells it was refreshing for me to know that deflection and small-talk are not necessary defaults. I have unfortunately failed to keep in touch with her, I suspect, in tribute to the sanctity of that conversation.

**

I like that when we go to the zoo in Patna, the cost of entry is 30 rupees (about 30¢) so, even for locals, going to the zoo does not feel like a major financial decision. The London zoo costs £21 – or 70 times the cost.

**

I have also been thinking a lot about the ways in which well-intentioned policies and practices end up having negative unintended consequences in adjacent domains. Or in other words, appreciating more concretely the influence of systems and "common practices" on the way we live and the things we therefore value.

For example, I've found that it's difficult to explain water waste to a man who uses a shower-head instead of a bucket. Things just don't quite compute. In India I would almost always shower with a bucket and a jug. This was not a conscious choice, but more a consequence of the fact that few bathrooms had showerheads, while almost all had a bucket. Now, a bucket might typically contain about 20L of water, whereas an average shower lasting 8 minutes will use around 65L. Because buckets were so much more available than showerheads in India, after getting accustomed to them, I would often prefer to use the bucket and jug even when a showerhead was available—it just felt more comfortable. The system inadvertently encouraged me to use less water.

There are other examples of this too—for example, how easy it is to be wasteful with plastic when in the UK, or Thailand, because it feels as though the whole society is set up to encourage the use of plastic. Because of food safety regulations and the like, so much of what we eat in England comes packaged in plastic. This ranges from loaves of bread in plastic wrapping, to biscuit packets, to hot chocolate powder. In India these kinds of things are definitely still available, but the difference is that when I go to the market to buy vegetables the man just throws everything—tomatoes, onions, mangoes, coriander, into one bag and I'm on my way. Almost never will I encounter individually wrapped apples, or 8 tomatoes in a plastic wrapped Styrofoam box like I do here in UK supermarkets. The point is that because of the way the entire system is set up, it is much easier to be less wasteful in India.

My Hindi speaking ability is not astounding, but it is enough to get me by. I can't use long words in Hindi. In Hindi, I don't know the word for elbow, or obfuscate, or hegemony, but I do know the words for arm, clear, and power, and so whenever my instinct is to talk in higher language or use SAT words, my language ability in Hindi pegs me back and I have to learn to express myself in simpler, more childlike language. I think about this in the light of academia—does using complex language cover over the central point being discussed, and only serve to exclude people who are not fluent in the dialect, or does it demonstrate a deeper understanding? Is it the case that speaking in simple language is an expression of higher understanding—if you can explain something to a five year old, then you clearly understand it very well; or is it that simple language introduces excess latency into conversations that can't get above a certain level until more complex, technical terminology is introduced?

I hope that one of the ways I've been changed by India is to simply care less about trivial things. I don't think so much about what other people are doing because I've been away from "other people" for so long. I've had to make so many decisions alone, and I've seen so many different kinds of people, and learned about the relative inconsequence of my decision making, that I now feel confident to go forward. I have also come to re-appreciate the value of the education I have received so far. There are many people in this world who cannot read English. There are many who have families to support, or parents to listen to, and who can't afford to do the kind of work I am now privileged enough to do. I ought to make the most of this.

A possible elephant in the room is that the real source of my confidence while in India I think comes from the way I am treated while in the country. For better or for worse, I'm tall, I'm foreign, I can get by in Hindi. I have a prestigious degree in a country where prestigious degrees are heavily over-valued (or else, one of the few means of escape) and so I am treated like a king here—sometimes I think I ought to act like it.

**

I rush down the steps to the river to get the last boat before the sun goes down. It's about 5 p.m. and this is when the last boat leaves. Twenty rupees to sit with 10 strangers for a minute and skirt across the 100m of river separating hippy-Hampi in the north from the UNESCO world heritage site Hampi in the south. I get to the other bank just in time to see the temple elephant going for his nightly walk. Elephants are majestic creatures. In the flesh they are sublime—a slab of cold hard mass; the stuff that stuff is made of—swaying gently from side to side in big waving gestures, ears flapping like liquid butterfly wings. I worry with each sway that the mass might fall over, and my, what an almighty crash that would make. The elephant is greeted the whole way by worshippers who touch him for a small blessing, and sometimes he will respond by tapping them on the head with his trunk. At dusk, he marches through the local town. The trainer lures him with a bell towards the stairs leading to the river, and the elephant with his huge mass and tree trunk legs does not miss a step the whole way down. I cannot be sure from the creature's eye position that he can see where he is going.

And then, the elephant keeps going; walks down the steps all the way into the river until his legs are wet, then his torso is in, and soon he is fully submerged under the water. It's elephant bathing time. He rolls around in the water like a happy beach ball, trunk breaking the surface sometimes and curling into a seahorse, accompanied by a loud snort. But the most striking visual is sheer size: A huge grey brown boulder, bobbing up and down in the twilight water.

**

I also learned this year just how much I enjoy being in rural places, where I can be in nature, and away from other people. In India I met a friend whose happiness can be measured as a function of how many people are around at the time—not in the Myers-Briggs sense that "I get my energy from people around me," or "I just need to be alone sometimes to recharge," but rather that she is visibly happier and mentally more sound when she isn't surrounded by a crowd of people. Perhaps this is a natural consequence of living in a country of more than a billion.

Occasionally, she would say things like "just look," swirling an arm in gesticulation at the crowds invariably in front of us. Privacy is hard won in India; the concept of personal space, and the invisible region around each of our bodies which we take for granted too often in the West does not exist in India. Both men and women will receive a pat down (in separate lines, India is still conservative enough) every time they get on a subway train in Delhi, and they won't let you on a plane until multiple men have touched your upper thighs to make sure you are not concealing anything. On some level this treatment is fair enough—India is one of the most at risk countries for terrorist attacks—and on another it is wholly uncomfortable to a society where personal space is prized.

I found that I quickly adjusted to the lack of private space. People will stand close on trains and public places. In Bihar, in shared rickshaws there are sometimes as many as 8 people squeezed thigh to thigh in a space that is designed to hold only 5. These people will often be complete strangers. When the auto rickshaw is full to the brim, the driver will happily invite you and two other people to sit up front with him and will contort himself and stretch his arms to be able to still steer the rickshaw. Often, the rickshaw will not leave until it is uncomfortably full – why not make an extra few rupees if you can!

**

I get into an auto-rickshaw and the driver looks to be about 14 years-old. A little young, but this is India, I don't bat an eye; I get in and we are on our way. Then, minutes into the journey he makes a manoeuvre which shoves us all to the right as he swerves to the left very suddenly—but this is India, I don't bat an eye; the traffic is always chaotic. It turns out though, that even in India cutting people off like this is considered bad form. I remember seeing the rat-toothed man behind us get off his motorbike, helmet still wrapped around his head, rushing over and barking down the side of the rickshaw. Paan stained teeth, mid-afternoon sweat; he grabs the kid by the collar and shouts profanities and saliva into his face for a whole minute: "Eh Kothiya! Look where you're going!" The boy eventually placates him with 300 (about $5) rupees and that's the end of the situation. The rat-toothed man walks away and we continue on our journey.

**

The highlight of my time in India was the two week period I spent in Bihar, to a place where not many foreigners are able to go. I visited at the invitation of Zubin Sharma and Project Potential—a group of incredible young people who are working to set up a rural university in India's poorest state. To get to where we were going, Kishanganj, in the North West of Bihar near the Nepalese border, we travelled for more than 28 hours, and I had to deal with a stranger tugging at my hair and asking if my afro was real.

As the train pulled in to the station we jumped up onto it while it was still moving and then forced open the locked doors so we could get our general class seats before the crowds came flooding in. When the first bus we were supposed to take was full, we unfolded the blankets we had packed in our bags and slept at the train station platform for a few hours. Then two more buses; each time the bus stations we transferred to had no solid floors, only mud, which we had to wade through to get to our spot. Most of the buses did not have numbers on them and there were no clear bays or signals for the bus to get onto. Instead, we had to listen closely over the noise of peanut and pineapple sellers, for the man standing in the front doorway of each bus screaming its destination as the bus was leaving the station. From that point on, it was our responsibility to make sure we were in the right place.

On the overnight train came one of the moments in India that really stood out for me. Sitting next to us was an astounding girl, maybe in her late teens or early twenties, who talked with us for almost three hours. She first injected herself into the conversation when she heard that we were talking about rural development, and that was an area she was interested in. But quickly, the conversation moved in a much more prescient direction as she told us about her experiences being a young woman living in rural India. "My father always called me "Beta"—the male version of something which might translate into English as child — she told us, making the point that her father treated her with the same level of respect as the males in her family. That she was not somehow less because she was a girl.

She spoke ferociously, her voice loud and confident as she talked about a whole range of issues. "Why is it that in the government service, 80% of jobs are reserved for men and only 20% for women!?" She was completely unintimidated by the fact that she was sitting in a crowded train compartment, while a crowd of middle-aged, dirty, tired looking men with piercing eyes and scowling faces were looking directly at her the whole time. "None of this will change," she continued, unfazed, "the way we treat women will not change, until we ourselves change our mindsets. The *people* are backwards."

When the conversation had calmed down and people began to leave the train, one of the men who had been staring for the whole interaction came and sat opposite of her and spoke to her directly—their noses only a foot or so apart. He scolded her, respectfully, that she was wrong about the country being backwards, and explained that what she called backwards was actually an important part of culture. But she was fully up to the challenge and responded to him calmly and forcefully.

It struck me that this is really how democracy ought to work. She was doing great work and if some of the people who were overhearing this conversation had their minds changed even a little by it, then her efforts had been worth it. She wasn't spending the train journey reading a book, or listening to music, she was using it to talk to people about some very difficult topics. It later emerged that though she was clearly from a very poor background, this young lady had been studying for a medical degree and then had to drop out when a member of her family got sick. I left the whole situation feeling like I had witnessed an act of great courage.

**

In Bihar the boys all slept on the floor in the same room where, during the day, we held our meetings. Eight people, each with only a single blanket, lay like dropped needles, in random directions across the padded floor.

**

Being in Bihar makes a person feel a little closer to the dirt, a little closer to the soil—the thing pigs roll around in, and the thing that feeds us. I don't like the evolutionary argument that humans evolved to live or not live a certain way because it is nostalgic, but there is something about the mechanical pace of life in modern day big cities that was brought into clearer focus after I had lived for a while in Bihar. In Bihar we wake up, we bathe, we eat, we work—never do we have to sit in a metal box for an hour to go through underground tunnels in order to brush past 3 million other people doing the same thing, to get to the ten or so people we actually work with on the 120th meter of a fully air conditioned building.

For me, there was an enlightenment that came from being put back in contact with the problems that modernity has supposedly liberated us from. There is an unmistakable joy in lighting a candle or telling stories in darkness because of a rainstorm outside. There is an unmistakable connection to nature that is achieved by walking miles and being blocked by water where bridges have not been built yet. And finally, I felt that there was a kind of humanisation that occurs when you have to do these basic things again for yourself – spending time preparing food from scratch, walking places, spending energy building relationships with local people even if only because they are the only ones who will be able to help you when things go wrong.

One day we awoke to news that a few kilometres away there had been severe flooding and that people needed help. This was not a big enough story to show up on international, or even national news, but we had heard stories that things were bad, and so we wanted to help. For much of our 7km walk, the surrounding landscape had been one of overfilled rice fields and the occasional house under a foot of water, but then it arrived. We heard it before we saw it. A free-flowing makeshift river that had popped up overnight and was flowing through a village and sweeping away everything in its path. The sight was enough to leave me flabbergasted. The fast flowing water seemed to be originating from a broad body of water receding further in the distance and collapsing into the horizon. The villagers told us that in the dry season, the river proper was more than 2km away, but because of the rains it had managed to gorge itself and make it to their doorsteps.

Though we went unprepared, we found that our good intentions were worth it. There were about 200 people stranded on the far bank of the river and we were able to make some phone calls to inform a rescue boat to go to them. This seems like a small task, and it was, but in places like rural flooded Bihar, there are no emergency services or firefighters. There are no news crews in helicopters encircling the site, trying to gauge where people are and helping them. It was just a group of villagers, mostly cut off from their friends in nearby villages, trying their best to keep dry and salvage what they can until the water goes away again. Hopefully our phone call meant that these people would not have to wait an extra day until someone came to pick them up.

Being in Bihar also taught me a huge amount about privilege, and its cousin, gratitude. One example of privilege showing up in an unexpected area is typing. I can type text at a rate that is not insufferably below my rate of thinking – I am not likely to give up on typing out a thought because doing so would involve finding letters on the keyboard at a pace that is too painfully slow for my brain to accommodate. It also means that I can find information much faster than someone who doesn't type—even if both of us have access to the internet and a computer. I can read webpages much faster than someone who is still learning English, or doesn't find themselves needing to use it every day.

Sometimes, this difference can be huge, to the point where it feels as though a person may need to make a commitment over several years before they are at a level where they can really benefit from the kinds of self-learning resources readily available to native English speakers (and the volume available in English versus other languages is huge). Relatedly, there is the privilege of having English as a first language. In Bihar it was a little strange at times to notice the juxtaposition between having a well-stocked library, written mostly in English, and a group of teenagers who mostly had not been taught to read English very well—people who were much more comfortable in their native tongues, or in Hindi, but there just isn't the same selection of books available in those languages.

One of the lessons I learned from spending time with Zubin is that at times where it seems as though you need to compromise your values, you may actually need to practice them harder. There was one very distinct moment in Bihar when we as a group were discussing the value of a university degree, and whether or not a degree was necessary. We noticed that there was a certain hypocrisy in preaching openly about how university degrees are flawed in fundamental ways; making people narrow minded. They impose certain narrow measures of success, they reward only a very particular type of learning, many people with university degrees don't know that much, but that many people in the group were still pursuing degrees while also participating in PPU.

During the discussion, I assumed that Zubin's line would be to argue somewhere near the middle ground—that he would take the view that for many of the participants of PPU, there were good reasons for them to continue with their more traditional education while also taking part in this new experiment. However, he took a different angle. Instead arguing that we should be consistent in what we preach and that if we say university degrees are not worth pursuing, then we should do our best not to pursue them. What this eventually led to was an in-depth discussion about university degrees and it seemed like many of the students were able to get far deeper into their thinking than if he had just taken the safe option.

The same lesson came up again when we were walking around Patna, trying to get a spontaneous meeting with a government official. Many of the security guards we came across seemed actively hostile at first, but as soon as Zubin told them about PPU and work we were doing, the vast majority of them commended him, and were happy to help in whatever way they could. Many of them offered good wishes, and commented that they felt the work being done by PPU was necessary and appreciated.

**

It is evening time and I am sitting on the top floor of our building in Bihar. There is no roof but the stars are hidden tonight. By day you can see for miles from here—miles and miles of farmlands turned rice paddies for the rainy season. To the side there is a small alcove in which we wash our dishes. The tap is waist high and there is no sink so the water and leftover rice pieces fall to the ground and drain away through a drainage groove cut into the concrete ground. I see a single raven swoop in and perch himself on the ledge overlooking the alcove. He has come for the food scraps, I think. He jumps down from the ledge and is now bang in the middle of food territory. Normally I might have stood up and shooed him away, but I am reminded of a concept from Vipassana meditation—"just observe, don't react." So I oversee, I watch him pit pattering; his neck impossibly flexible as he jits and juts his eyes all around. I worry he will move into the bathroom next door, in which case he will be much more difficult to remove. Maybe he will make his nest in there, and scare the next person who needs to pee. Another raven arrives, perches himself on the ledge and caws, wide mouthed, as though calling for reinforcements, I am worried, a little, for no justifiable reason—maybe the raven will make his way into the kitchen where the real food lives. The benefits of observing though, is that I start to see things. I see the ledge raven walking to and fro like an army general, his shoulders hunched up, marching in short, pointed steps. When he is still I see that he looks statesman-like, with a thick neck and broad chest. When he finally leaves I see that even he has to deal with the fact of his own bulk. That his wings are not graceful, they flap violently, vigorously. That when the second raven flies, he first falls, momentarily, towards the Earth and has to pull himself, torrid, upwards.

**

Upon returning to the UK, and then visiting the US, I noticed how suddenly and how quickly everything changed. I had spent much of my time in India actively avoiding documentation and specifically trying to escape the pattern of doing things because they promised to be good conversation topics—and yet here, that was all I seem to be judged by. Questions I previously had no need to answer were now suddenly being made into a priority. I was being asked well-intentioned questions like what the "three highlights" of my India experience were, or "what did I learn?" As if it were somehow possible to distill a year's worth of experience into a nice bite-sized chunk; that the person I was talking to could somehow get a window into my experience without ever having lived through the experience himself. The whole reason I travelled to India in the first place was in service to the idea that this kind of experience is not possible to live vicariously. You had to have been there, you had to have seen it with your own eyes.

**

I feel the need now to be rooted to a place. I would like to be able to make promises to people; I would like to be able to make commitments to things, and to be unable to get out of those commitments no matter how hard I try.

That place is somewhere closer to courage.

**

BACK IN LONDON

When I originally set out on my journey, I imagined that I would travel forever. I fantasised about the idea of being a truly global citizen who could live a wholesome life with no more than what he could carry on his back. I hoped that I would be able to earn money while travelling and find a way to make slow, long-term travel sustainable. I even thought about what it might be like to eventually raise children on the road—that maybe a child who has seen everything would have the broadest possible worldview, and would be better off for it. However, after spending almost 15 months travelling, I felt I had learned what I needed, and the value of continuing travel was diminishing.

I was troubled, for example, by the fact that I could no longer make commitments to people. Since I did not know where I would be a month, or three months from now, it was difficult for me to involve myself in a community for long enough to develop deep relationships, and be truly useful. Occasionally, I did fall immediately into a deep friendship, and those friendships I still treasure to this day, but the time together always ended too soon and it is difficult to have a view towards building in such situations. A tree would likely never lay down roots if it knew it was going to be moved in a few weeks.

The traveller's lifestyle I was living was also starting to feel incredibly selfish. In most of the places I visited, I felt like I was taking away more than I was giving back, primarily because I was a guest, and by virtue of my presence in a place, I was asking to be accommodated. I felt that all this consumption could not be truly justified unless I could find a way to contribute also, and contribution seemed to require being rooted to a single place for some time. Quite often, all that other people need from you is that you stick around. There is an argument to be made that by travelling for some period of time, you become much more useful to the people you do eventually connect with, by virtue of your broadened experience, and I was coming to the point where the scales were tipping away from moving and towards staying.

I had to pick a place to call home, and I decided to choose the oldest of all the possible choices: the place where I had grown up, and where my family still was, London.

My plan was that I would find a community in London and that I would try my best to be part of it. To engage in a way that I had been unable to while I was moving frequently from place to place. I decided that I would get a job and try to improve my skills and that I would step forward into adulthood (assuming that my travels had been an extended adolescence) with conscious intention and determination.

The day I landed back in London, I took a familiar journey on the tube home from the airport. The sky was dripping with rain, as it always seems to in London, and the colour of everything, not just the clouds, was a muted grey. I felt like an alien. The sentiment crystallised when I got to West Ham station and heard, over the tannoy, "Due to adverse weather conditions the floor may be slippery. Please take extra care when walking around the station." My first thought was that "adverse weather conditions," was an awfully long-winded way to say "It's raining." My second was that I felt horribly infantilised. I had just come from a place where the trains often did not have doors; even while the train was moving full-speed the passengers would be hanging half-and-half out the side. On public buses people would climb onto the roof and sit cross-legged for the duration of the journey. In London, the "mind the gap" messages suddenly felt demeaning—I didn't need a tannoy system to tell me not to slip on a wet floor, I had eyes to see with, and I wasn't a five year old. My natural instinct for survival should be enough to ensure I don't fall into the gap between the train and the platform, thank you very much.

On that train journey, the Jubilee Line from West Ham, everything in London felt clean to the point of being sterile. I felt like I was in a hospital under constant supervision. People seemed to be dressed impeccably and I couldn't imagine how long they had spent that morning to look so sharp. I couldn't imagine how many times the well-groomed man had looked in the mirror before he stepped out of his house. I suddenly noticed all the spots, tears and mud-marks on my own clothing. Everyone seemed to be in their own heads, listening to music, or playing games on their phones. It was a very surreal experience. The reverse culture shock of returning to London was significantly larger than the shock of leaving had been.

My thoughts on London have progressed since those first impressions and now I believe, unfortunately, that I have some more sinister critiques.

The writer, Ta Nahesi Coates argues that if you want to understand what a society values, then you should look at the policies it instantiates and assume that the results of those policies are intentional. By such a judgement, London seems to inordinately favour the rich and the old. House prices in London are famously so high that you have to be a Russian Oligarch, a Saudi Prince or a Chinese business tycoon to own property within the city. If I take Ta Nahesi Coates's advice seriously then it is clear that what London loves most is banking and finance. The salaries in the banking sector are rungs above other industries (almost all the jobs listed on my university careers website in London were in finance) and as a result, many of the best students and most ambitious people go on to jobs in finance. As an indirect consequence of this, so many decisions in London have become financial decisions. The cost of living in the centre of London is high enough that most young people live far away from each other, so seeing friends for a casual hang-out requires advanced planning. There are very few free, public spaces to socialise and so meeting friends entails a non-trivial payment to some restaurant or bar. In India I could feed myself with 25p plates of rice and lentils; in London it was impossible to get a burger for less that £6.

When I returned to London it was the autumn of 2016, and I expected that there would be a war on. The EU referendum vote had happened 6 months prior and I presumed the 'Battle of Brexit' to be raging and that the generals would be in need of as many soldiers as they could find. Instead what I discovered was apathy. I found people to be relatively placid, and defeated, at least in comparison to the civic energy I had seen in India. I cannot blame anyone, because soon after I started my job in London I took on the same routines that everyone else had—wake up, commute, work, lunch, commute, dinner, sleep—it left very little room for civic action or involvement. I also found that life in London was organised around long established institutions, and I think part of my malaise during this period was that I felt I did not have access to those core institutions. I had not been to Oxford or Cambridge, I was not receiving invitations to the talks and film screenings happening in London's numerous private members' clubs.

I later learned that there was a battle going on but it was happening in silence, and Britain was losing. The battle was within the country, a battle between young and old, a battle between those with capital and those without, and a battle conducted with sanitised language and repeated phrases. In India, my Hindi was at only a conversational proficiency, so I was forced to remain at the level of simple and easily understood ideas. In Hindi, I did not know the words for "hegemony" or "platitude" or "elbow". The joy of India though, was that I never had to deal with meaninglessly bloated phrases like "hesitate to contact", "create a dialogue", "open a conversation", "to whom it may concern", "community", "break down barriers", "Brexit means Brexit", "the best possible deal"—phrases, which in England, seemed to be the bulk of the public discourse.

I haven't been able to write very much since returning to London, for two reasons. Firstly, that there is already too much writing out there, and secondly because I have nothing to say. My life for the past year, despite being at a wonderful company where I am learning an incredible amount and am around great people, has been thoroughly dull. My computer screen looks the same day after day, and I spend day after day in front of it. I can type faster now. If my memories from India feel broad and vibrant, the year since I arrived in London has been squashed, by virtue of repetition, into just a sliver in my memory.

The one major highlight from the time I have spent in London though, is Newspeak House. A building, and group of people in East London who embody so many of the principles and ideals I was looking for when I returned from my travels. Every Wednesday evening there is a communal dinner, cooked by one of the resident fellows, and anyone from the wider community is invited to join, eat, socialise and meet new people. I am incredibly grateful for all the friends I have made at Newspeak. That place has been a real beacon of light for me over the past two years.